An Oakwoods Almanac

Other works by Gerry Loose include

Change (images by K. Sweeney McGee)
Yuga Night (with Larry Butler & Kathleen McGee)
Knockariddera
a measure
Eitgal
Being Time
The Elementary Particles
Tongues of Stone
Printed on Water — New & Selected Poems *
the deer path to my door
that person himself *
fault line

as editor

The Holistic Handbook
Seed Catalogue (with Morven Gregor)
Ten Seasons: explorations in botanics
        (with photographs by Morven Gregor)

as editor & translator

The Botanical Basho (with Yushin Toda)

Shearsman titles

Gerry Loose

An Oakwoods Almanac

with photographs by
Morven Gregor

Shearsman Books

Published in the United Kingdom in 2015 by
Shearsman Books Ltd
50 Westons Hill Drive
Emersons Green
BRISTOL
BS16 7DF

Shearsman Books Ltd Registered Office
30-31 St. James Place, Mangotsfield, Bristol BS16 9JB
(this address not for correspondence)

www.shearsman.com

ISBN 978-1-84861-435-2

Copyright © Gerry Loose, 2015.
Images copyright © Morven Gregor, 2015.

The right of Gerry Loose to be identified as the author of this work
has been asserted by him in accordance with the
Copyrights, Designs and Patents Act of 1988.
All rights reserved.

Acknowledgements
Parts of this book were first published in *A Wilder Vein* (ed Linda Cracknell, Two Ravens Press 2009) under the title 'Ardnamurchan Almanac'; in *Earthlines*, Sylva Caledonia catalogue and others in the online journal *Gists and Piths*.

I am grateful for a Creative Scotland Award and a Kone Foundation Residency at Saari Manor, which allowed me time to live in the woods and to both start and finish this book.

My gratitude is also extended to those friends who read and commented on this book as it was being written: Peter Manson, Tom Leonard, Gerrie Fellows, Maggie Graham, Larry Butler; and above all, my partner, Morven Gregor.

In memory of the hound, Dharma, who asked no questions.

Contents

One

Sunart.................7

Two

Saari................99

One

Sunart

2007

September 21st

I'm given an unexpected release of tears this morning. On the CD player, I'm playing Verdi's *Requiem*, with Ezio Piza and Beniamino Gigli, the great tenor of his day. The formality of the Latin verse, in the Italian pronunciation, suggestive as the words of a lover. Piza's profound bass rolls in the low and rocky Ardnamurchan hills. I listen to the *Dies Irae* and "the trumpet scattering wonderful sound" and I'm moved. The words and music reach into me to find something I didn't know was there, and the *Quid sum miser*: "Who am I, wretched man, to say, whom ask to intercede, when the just man is barely safe?" forces what's inside to my eyes.

Recorded in August 1939, with the full atrocities of another miserable war breaking.

I heard the day's news: Israeli planes in Syria, soldier killed in Helmand explosion, UK to retain certain types of cluster bombs, US private contractors open fire randomly in Iraq; fundamentalists killing each other and us. How do I reconcile this requiem – a plea to a god in whom I can't believe – with holy wars? I can take no more and turn off the actual music, pull on my boots and hat, walk out and up the hill.

Every day here at Gobsheallach, I visit the wood ant colonies. They are in a dip in the road, a single track. To the north, ascending the hill, are thin birches and wind-broken small oaks, all sitting among mosses and ferns and outcrops of rock emblazoned with lichen circles. To the south, where the burn gathers force, are alders, whose first spring growth had a fine papal and sexual purpling.

These little colonies – for they are little, unlike those classic ziggurats on the other side of the bay at the edge of the sitka plantation – have grown despite the maniac flailings of the hedging and verging machine, which, during the growing seasons, periodically demolishes their citadels. But their colonies survive. I don't know what will become of the other communities when the plantation over there is clear felled. I love these ants. They are Scottish wood ants, *Formica aquilonia* (though this colony of perhaps a hundred thousand may be *Formica lugubris*. There is plenty to mourn). *Seangan*, in Gaelic, the noun common to all ants: pismire; this one's a fairly large ant with a dark head and abdomen and red thorax. Scarce in most of Britain, though as its name might imply, apparently plentiful here. Her work is never over. One mound is on the flat into soft earth, with bracken shading from the heat of the summer sun. Another is built on a rock outcrop. Here, at some point, a portion has slid off the slanting surface some three feet, to land, broken, on another pointed rock below. Upon this rock I will build. These ants move nest-building detritus, broken bracken and leaf fragments, from the lower wreckage of their city to the upper, to rebuild their labyrinths of underground chambers and grottoes. Maeterlinck, the Belgian playwright (later, Count Maurice Polydore Marie Bernard Maeterlinck), in his 1930 *The Life of the Ant*, writes of their architecture: "…in the ants' nest we should find the horizontal style predominant, with innumerable and apparently aimless meanderings, an endless extent of catacomb cities, from which none of us, were they built upon our scale, would ever emerge."

Maeterlinck's earlier book, *The Life of the White Ant* was a plagiarism of Eugene Marais' *The Soul of the White Ant*. Marais, a South African poet, scientist and morphine addict killed himself with a shotgun as a result.

All summer I've watched them at their task. Today is overcast, threatening rain; the temperature is dropping, but still there are ants walking backward up three feet of bare rock overhang. I track one: she's hefting a fragment of dried bracken four times her own length, as she ascends, never pausing, scaling a height thirteen hundred times her own: *her* height, since she is female and since I have seen others standing almost erect, caressing each other with their antennae, communicating what's unknowable to me. The three feet of the rock, though, isn't much when considering that most of their foraging is done in the birch and oak canopy many times this height. Here they milk sap-feeding bugs, like the aphid *Symydobius oblongus*, of their honey dew, which is drawn down by a gentle stroking; the honey dew, rich in sugars and vitamins, is the aphid's natural waste matter. This aphid is lovingly tended like any prize buttermilk-rich cow. The ants, as well as farming aphids, tend their pastures. They prey on herbivorous insects, sawflies and moths, which, unchecked, could soon deplete the tree pastures they feed on.

This climbing ant, in four minutes, as near as I can tell, has reached the upper city and disappeared into a newly made doorway, away from the prevailing rain. For now the rain has started. The queens here are moving into autumnal diapause, stopping their production of eggs, which have been laid unceasingly since their spring nuptial flight. The flying males are allowed their moment of ecstasy, then die. Requiem; then hibernation. I stare out across the bay where the tide is ebbing away. Above, two hooded crows veer lazily away as they spot me. Something unseen, perhaps a heron, shrieks on Eilean Dubh, the black island, one of the two conjoined tidal islands in the Atlantic gate of the bay's mouth.

On the walk back to my cottage, the rain on my face, I gather enough chanterelles for my supper, together with some deer-nibbled birch bolete to dry for stock. There is a dead shrew, perfect on the metalled road, left to lost unstrung rosaries of sheep droppings.

Inter oves locum praesta, sings Gigli – Grant me a place among the sheep.

25th

who decrees decay
allows for growth

The little fly, *meanbh-chuileag, Culicoides impunctatus*, needs blood for its life cycle, which it draws unasked through its rolled mouthparts from mammals unfortunate enough to be in its vicinity. This, on lower, wetter ground in Ardnamurchan, is most of us who venture outside; with one hectare (about the size of a shinty field) reckoned to host to as many as 24 million larvae of that particular fly.

The adults draw energy more acceptably from flowers' nectar, but it's also a detritivore, feeding on rotting vegetation. Among its predators are the insectivorous plants – sundews and butter-worts, but even together with others – dragonflies, swifts, pipistrelles, palmated newts and the common lizard, these cannot keep pace with the sheer numbers of these midges with their bloodsucking habits.

Round about now, the midges begin to fade away, adults dying off in the colder, wetter and windier weather that's blowing in after the autumnal equinox. They are generally all gone by October. The final instar of the larva, however, overwinters in the ground, making sure of species continuance and mammal discomfort (mainly deer and humans) next year. The females, it seems, smell our breath and the presence of lactic acid. The first bite, and taste of blood, and she'll release pheromones to attract her sisters. Maybe the answer is to neither take milk nor to breathe. Nobody has ever recorded dead vegans being bitten.

The disappearance of the midge happens at the same time as the migration of the martins that flickered over and round the byres all summer. Here in Gobsheallach, the martins' nesting sites had been disturbed by recent building works and the prowling cats, but having flown for up to three months from sub-Saharan Africa to get here, they don't give up easily. With the hills changing from purple to brown, though, they're away south again, apparently landing long enough to rest and then make the dangerous journey maybe fifteen thousand miles north, a hundred and sixty odd miles a day, to arrive in time to help eat midges.

Bluetongue fits into my imagination somewhere between bluestocking and the nose of a permanently and amiably confused drinker. The bluetongue virus could affect the other controversial mammals in these parts, along with foot and mouth: sheep. Although the virus has so far been found in the UK only in a part of England, maybe five hundred miles from here, the Department for Environment, Food and Rural Affairs (Defra) estimates that the midge which spreads this virus (the same genus as the *meanbh-chuileag*) can travel maybe a mile a day; "However, if caught in suitable meteorological conditions midges can be carried much farther distances, especially over water masses, i.e. more than 200 kms (124 miles)". Bluetongue virus was first described in South Africa, coincidentally where "our" housemartins have been recorded landing.

Sheep here are practically as wild as the deer they share the hill with. Although, safely grazing on sea grasses and on the tidal islets in the bay, the small black Hebridean sheep and their sometimes piebald lambs are approachable enough. As is Charley, the one-eyed tup, who wants only to overwinter in my kitchen; drink my malt for all I know. Difficult to control, then. I've seen crofters, aunties, uncles and postmen pressed into service, with dogs sometimes hindering the gathering for shearing or dipping, all running and shouting across the sands, over the thrift and campion, re-enacting somehow a Keystone comedy. The midges, though, have no such trouble with sheep or deer.

Another sort of clearing of the land, again with financial subtexts, may soon afflict people here. The advent (coming with the wind) of the bluetongue midge, neither amiable nor at all literary may take up where unscrupulous landlords left off.

The Sunart show, just after the first foot-and-mouth movement restriction orders this summer, was a sad affair: no sheep or cattle. A wet west Highland day, with only a hectoring Loch Lomondside farmer displaying his sheepdogs' skill in herding (flocking?) ducks from one part of the central ring to another, not once but twice.

Ardnamurchan, described in one unsuccessful attempt to attract tourists as "almost an island", jutting as it does with its odd rhino head into the Atlantic between Mull and the small isles of Rum, Eigg, Muck and Canna, its eye a ring-dyke of volcanic origin, is most definitely not an island – as if water were in any case a safeguard from viruses.

The commonwealth of martins and the interlocking communities of deer, humans and midges ebb and flow. With the midges and the martins, the motor-homes move at their stately pace along the single track roads, southing, overwintering, perhaps, with bluetongue midges. Their place in local economy is debated; with a former B&B crofter (her croft sits among one of the best examples of Sunart oakwoods) speaking of their coming into the area coinciding with the decline of her business. As they depart, the other caravan dwellers return – the travellers are back in Glen Tarbert – a glen of winter deer. The travellers were here long before the holidaying motor home-owners; before the feudal-minded industrialists who bought sporting estates in the late nineteenth century. Alastair Cameron, in his "Annals and Recollections of Sunart" records their spring arrival (together with the long disappeared "milestone inspectors") in the first decade of the twentieth century: "it was nothing unusual for me on my way home from school to meet three or four squads of them with their carts and horses. Stewarts, Macmillans, Johnstones, Williamsons, and up till 1908 or thereabouts, Browns and Wilsons were the most regular." They were kindly received, with their tales and tinware.

People cleared for sheep; sheep cleared for deer; conceivably deer and sheep both giving way to a virus; travellers yielding to tourists. Depopulation continues.

26th

It's just after the equinox. Tonight it's full moon – the harvest moon. This moon rises due east and sets due west. The length of a day is equal to the length of a night, but night, a cockstep at a time, is catching me unawares each twilight. There's a threshold here. From here I can stare into winter. It makes me edgy seeing the blackness in this morning's brilliant sun, reflected in the little pools of last night's rain left among rushes. Today's tides will be high and already the bay is preparing itself, with a calmness in the dazzle of sun, for the tons of water which will later pour in to cover its cold sands. The clouds are piled high to the south. Bare rock outcrops on the slopes glimmer, blink back in an unaccustomed brightness. Peat hags hold their water like the toothless crones they are, only tufts of bog cotton above on skinny stems. Pismires are slow today, stunned by the cold westerly. Ben Resipole's eastern flank hunkers in shadows. The last bee is at the last scabious flower.

27th

It's harder than that. I said I'd go to the woods. Send words back. Maybe one at a time. And then the meter reader comes and he's too short. Oak. There's one word. It's a hard word. The words are metered too. Maybe I should spit them out fast: oak, alder, aspen, birch, holly. No elder yet. Maybe that's what's holding me back. No elders. We must invent it all for ourselves, just as they told us. Is it the aspens trembling in the wind or the rain hissing on the sea at Ardtoe? Pine. I can't read all the leaves of this wooden book. Instead I must add to them. How fortunate to be born human and see the leaves turn from those green shades to yellows and reds and all on the same pillar. And to smell the moulded centuries underfoot, cladding the jutting bedrock.

Then a friend calls so we talk of apple trees instead.

29th

It's also hard for me to walk about here and return with nothing in my pockets. It's frequently a leaf or a blossom for a jug or jar on the table. There are so many shades of green. Today it's three little red apples and a conker. The conker is small and is probably one overlooked by everyone else; not that many children pass this way. Adults don't bother. Conkers have the rich sheen of polished furniture. They glow in the afternoon sun. They're wealth with no work on my part, and I'm always reminded of Bashō giving the horse chestnuts of Kiso as presents to city folk. Sometimes this comes out in translation as acorns. It's the present of that autumnal wealth that's important, not the form it takes. Bashō is saying, with his simple gift, the very obvious: here's true riches. The apples are

tiny – from wilding trees, small, spherical and deep red. What promise; of course as bitter as sloes. But in cooking, they'll be transformed. What delights of apple jelly they'll make, together with the long greeny-yellow apples whose pronounced separate base, a swelling upwards, is like cumulus gathering. Those came last week, stuffed in my pockets from the tree no-one bothers about on the road to Ariundle. How can I pass over the fruits of trees' labour? They shine three times. Once in the finding, once in the cooking and at last, in the greedy devouring and savouring.

Pome: the characteristic fruit of the apple family, as an apple, pear, or quince, in which the edible flesh arises from the greatly swollen receptacle and not from the carpels.

How many years since I first read Joyce's *Pomes Penyeach*? I take it from the shelf and read from 'A Memory of The Players in a Mirror at Midnight', written in Zurich in 1917:

> *Pluck forth your heart, saltblood, a fruit of tears.*
> *Pluck and devour!*

October
4th

I should have written: zealots, followers of the Word given, sent down; not *fundamental*-ists, since there is nothing of essence about them.

Away for a couple of days in Galloway and the Ariundle apples on the cherry boards of my desk have moved from deepsea to lit suns, with a rouged blush. The leaf-chart of bloods and wines, amber and umber, golds and saffron is again surrendering to the pull of earth and its gravity, its gravitas and its fun. The odd flashpoint colour of a sycamore branch, its leaves no longer producing chlorophyll, green as the days shorten, moving beyond equinox towards solstice. Autumn always climbs sycamores a limb at a time, while the rowan's tinted, tinged everywhere. A mirror to the rowan's berries is in the scarlet dogrose hips, beamed forth and back, a recognition, a signal: the way light seduces.

In October sun Glen Tarbert wears a thick new pelt the colour of a fox. The sky's not quite the blue of a kingfisher, but this is already a halcyon day. A passing dozy buzzing fly lands on my eyebrow and I wink. I remove the fly and wink again at the conspiracy of the day.

In his poem 'Why I Am Not a Painter', Frank O'Hara, not thinking of autumn, writes: "There should be / so much more, not of orange, of / words, of how terrible orange is / and life."

Terrible perhaps, in the sense of trembling, of intensity. Certainly, the hound beside me feels it and trembles in the face of it moving around us with an intensity that drives all the woodlands, all its creatures.

This hound is a graceful and supple animal, taller than a roe deer.. She is a constant companion, one who makes no demands except that companionship she freely offers. We suit each other: she'll not walk unless invited, preferring rather to lie at full stretch. In fact, being lean, angular and long-limbed – bred to run, to the chase – she cannot sit down like a mere dog. She must either stand or lie down. She aristocratically ignores all dogs as a peregrine ignores the small flyting birds that scold. She'll not bark except for very good reason. We are silent together in contemplation of the vastness of night. Canes venatici.

Tonight, somewhere over towards Creag Dhubh and the little lochans in the hills, Laga and Lochan Sligneach, the stags are bellowing. The Milky Way is all that lights our path, and the winking lights and long drone of the black plane in the dark where no airline flies.

We return, the hound and myself, to a phone message from a friend on his way to Syria, one place of his former imprisonment and torture. He's asking for my prayers. Palestinian, Muslim, stateless, lately an imam in his own play, hating imams, he says, all imams. In my prayerless fashion, I respond watchfully: a bat, probably a pipistrelle, just the one, flittering and swooping, looping over and over hard by the old rowan with its knuckled roots gripping rock outcrop.

5th

At the jetty and along, by the little wooden boathouse, there's no blue and white china fragments on the shore. The crackling blue shining of the mussel shells deceives, though. And the insides of dog whelks on the rocks, broken possibly by crows, are quietly luminescent, faint mauve and nicotine-yellow spiralling chambers. Fish jump clear of the water here, almost beneath the Miocene other-world gaze of the black cormorants on their rock, twenty four in this colony, unmoving; watching wind against the tide. The small creel boats at moorings swing and fall and rise. The parchment grey-black leaves of aspens rattle onto the shore. Acorns drop and roll into the sea. It's how the brindled hound and I measure each day's incursion into another season.

6th

It's easy to make out the warp and weft of society here, how bards and poets are fabric, along with genealogists and story tellers. They're in fact often the same person anyway, and there's little distinction between personal history and society's doings, real or imagined. Alec Dan Henderson, of Acharacle, an uncle of my landlady, in conversation with Donald Archie MacDonald, in 1967, as recorded in Tocher, discusses local folk of the time of the clearances: "The people were cleared away from Ardnamurchan. And he climbed out by Beinn Shianta and saw the places where the people used to be, and the old walls which were left. There was nobody there." The *he* in this is the Doctor of Rahoy, one Dr John MacLachlan, a poet of whom Sorley MacLean writes: "…your back was strong and straight / as you went up the face of Ben Shianta / with the burden on your shoulders / of seeing the land a waste / under sheep and bracken and rushes." Alec Dan, although not a young man in 1967, may not have met John MacLachlan, who died at seventy years of age in 1874, but his memory is strong, and he sings a song from someone who had it from the Doctor of Rahoy: *Direadh a-mach ri Bein Shianta*; Climbing up Beinn Shianta. The doctor no doubt knew the Ben when its lower slopes were inhabited. The song has a verse: "And d'you think you'll find peace, with your sheep and your cattle-folds?" addressing "Grey-headed MacColl of the evil deeds" who put out the people from their place. In the same poem [Dr John MacLachlan (of Rahoy in Morvern)] Sorley MacLean also writes of "The Cameron in Bun Allt Eachain, / that rare knowledgable man, / he told about a gleam of the sun / on beautiful Morvern / in the time of its emptying and its misery." The Cameron, Alasdair Cameron, a road man, wrote elegantly in both English and Gaelic. Bun Allt Eachain is where I was walking yesterday, driven there by Alasdair Cameron's little book "Annals and Recollections of Sunart", published in 1961, in which he writes of the nearby Tigh-na-Caillich: [which] "commemorates landlord despotism, which made a harmless old woman the victim of a son's indiscretion. Why? Oh why, one may ask, should the iniquity of the son be visited on the mother – particularly when he did punishment for his crime of stealing a sheep." I was looking for the "solitary Scots pine tree, a lone sentinel which has braved many a blast" at Bun Allt Eachain; but it was gone. Later I spoke to a man in Strontian who had known Alastair Cameron, or "North Argyll", his pseudonym, or "North" as he was affectionately known.

The Doctor of Rahoy, born in 1804, sees the results of mid-century clearance and makes a song. The song is sung in Ardnamurchan and Morvern, where it's heard by Alec Dan Henderson and passed on; The doctor's story is told, also in the middle of a new century, by one of the greatest Gaelic poets. (MacLean's note to his own poem: "Dr John MacLachlan was one of the best Gaelic poets of the nineteenth century") MacLean also remembers the knowledge of the road man, Alasdair Cameron of Bun Allt Eachan, where I look for a Scots pine. The Annals and Recollections in its language, its feeling for people and its democracy of greatness, is as neat an encapsulation of the last 200 years in the memory of Gaels as may be found.

That long memory is abroad in this parish today in other matters – the writing of a letter apparently questioning the mental faculties of another doctor of medicine, the calling to the General Medical Council, and "enforced" resignation. The consequences of that letter divided the usually polite co-existing communities here. There may be many odious reasons for clearances and more yet for sad and bitter resignations; but those who clear are not forgotten. Painted signs, nailed to oaks and chestnut trees, hung from deer grids and rock faces read "We support Dr Buchanan" all across the two peninsulas. Recently new signs have been hung: "Backstabbers Your Day Will Come" and the single word: "Traitor".

7th

Hill farming economics, 2007: Scottish Government subsidy per lamb slaughtered and incinerated: £15. ["a welfare disposal scheme to slaughter and render up to 250,000 light lambs that would normally be exported, but which are stuck on Scottish farms and now in an unmarketable condition because of the export ban and livestock movement restrictions"]. Abattoir prices in Dingwall: (200 mile round trip from Ardnamurchan, includes ferry) for slaughter, £17 per lamb. Slaughtered, butchered and dressed, total per lamb, £30. (Cost to farmer). No local buyers for lamb (and certainly not mutton, despite aristocratic and chef noises off). Wethers at market: £2 – £3. Wool: no market value. Cost of lamb chops in supermarket: £3.67 per kilo. Cost of grassland, per acre, per lamb, unknown. Cost of supplementary feeding, variable, but expensive. From

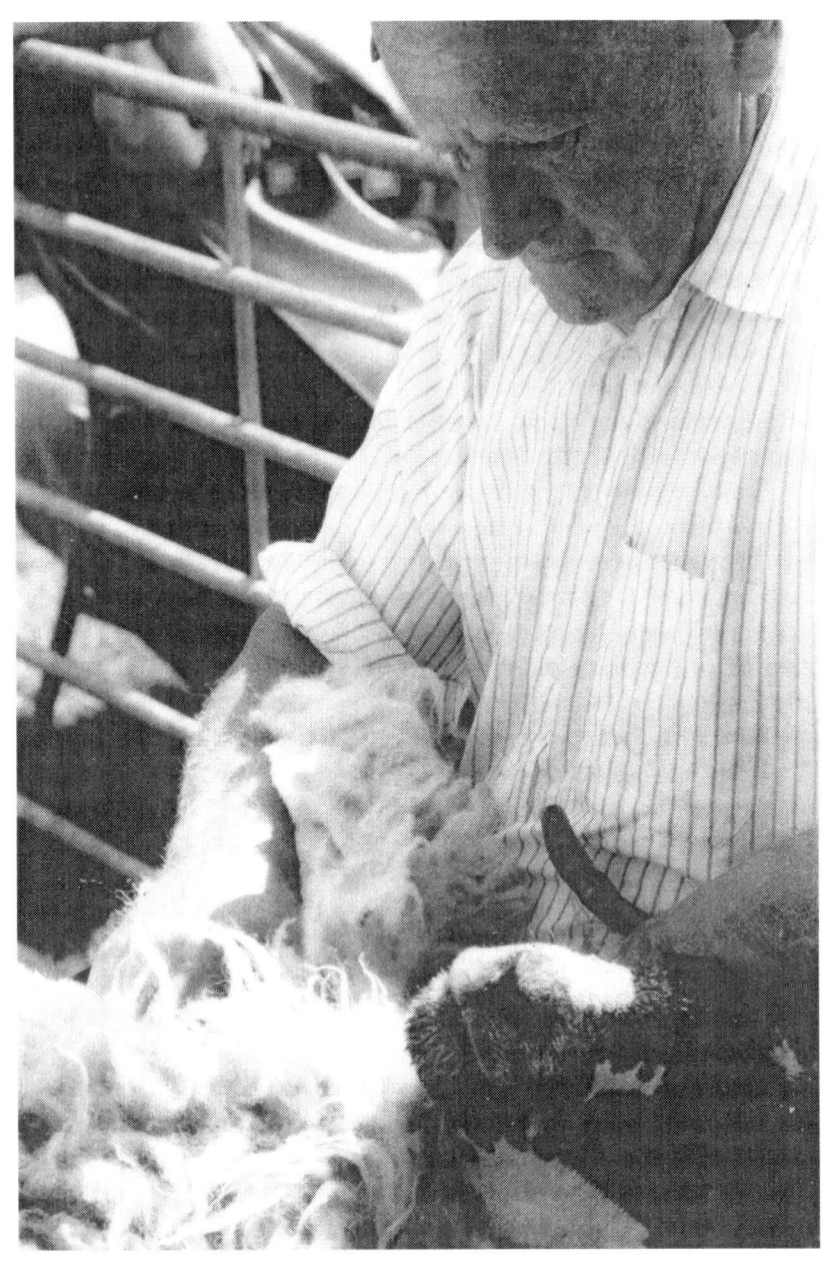

The Herald (October 6 2007): "The Northern Ireland Red Meat Industry Task Force, established to develop a five-to-ten-year strategy for the beef and sheep-meat industry has concluded that suckler-origin beef and hill sheep have no future. The report also concluded that it is not possible to create an economically viable production model for an efficient producer of hill sheep unless the farmgate price increases substantially to approximately £2.80 per kilo. Such conclusions are just as relevant to Scottish producers and will set alarm bells ringing in an industry already in crisis from the foot-and-mouth and blue tongue outbreaks."

8th

All morning Ben Resipole, Creag Dhubh, Bein Bhreac and the others can't rise from the clouds. There's no Sgurr visible to the west, no pointed Viking hills of Rum – Hallival, Askival, no Ainshval to be seen. The hound lies heraldic on the heather. Over by the parish church they slash and burn rhododendron understorey, but the smoke cannot clear the canopy, tangles in branches. Sheep amble past on their journey into the subconscious. While the mist hides, it also reveals: vast moorlands of webs, each with points of water at each intersection. There are two types of spiderweb here – one is floss and largely horizontal, but with diagonal digressions and sometimes seemingly random. This is all across the bog myrtle and up high into pale birches. The other kind is the geometric spiral from one branch to another of the oak and the rowan. The spiders must have (over millennia) adjusted web building techniques to what they hoped to catch, if hope is not too far-fetched a notion in the case of a spider. Like any fisherman, the mesh is larger or smaller according to the anticipated haul. Mist also amplifies the often unheard, the unlistened to: the booming surge of the incoming tide and the crescendo of curlews. From all directions, the stags' great groans of existence, their moaning lust for life driving them. Electricity volts through the hound's lead to my hand; she's seen them first – a stag and three hinds making unhurriedly for higher ground. Her ancestors sing in her blood, she trembles lightly. In another life I would have slipped her after them and followed her uphill.

9th

To walk across the coruscating mile of the bay in October sun, between land and clear sky, is to walk on rippling quicksilver. A heron stares at a limpid and disappearing rock pool. The pure, bubbling, unworded call of flighting curlews curves down to my ear. Halfway across I'm a tiny figure in reflected light, walking, walking, just one foot before the other.

a brindled hound
a lichened oak

Inside a wood, it is hard to see it for the trees which overwhelm with their forms, twisted, broken, growing one in the other. The curling holly finds shelter in the oak, rowans crawling decade on decade round the rocks send out more roots, grip tighter, a birch trunk springs back on itself in a slow double bend; a complete alphabet, a language of forms and lives. I find it hard also to see the trees for this reason. It's infinitely more complicated by the lichens and mosses. Mosses are knee deep in places and year on year take themselves further up into the trees. Where the mosses are not in evidence, the lichens bubble across trunks. Ferns, too, in the crooks formed by the reaching out of limbs. and of course, the old nurse trees will have saplings growing in them. Sometimes it's possible to see what appears to be two or even three types of leaf on the one tree until the intertwining trunks, like ivies, can be separated from the moss and the ferns by the recalcitrant eye.

In places where we wander, say at Sailean nan Cuileag, the inlet of flies, there's no such problem for the hound. She's suddenly there ahead of me on the path, her eyes undeceived and undeceiving, she follows me, now to the east, then the west, ahead, behind, plaiting around me like a sapling alongside a veteran oak. She's perfectly disguised for this woodland, soft footed, and in the October colours and light, all but invisible in her fur lines of broken amber and darker brown. We don't take the same path – she has long delicate limbs, built for the speed of the chase, which would catch in the cracks of those mossy rockfaces I scramble up and down – but we end up in the same place – she's a gaze hound: from within her grace she can see my upright lumbering form as surely as I see the bunching leathery lungwort on the oak trees we pass.

10th

FISH PRICES

Fleetwood – 22,500 kilos on the market. Witches 30p-£1; monkfish £2-£3.80; flounder 20p-60p each.

Fraserburgh – 14 boats landed 1,005 boxes. Monkfish £90-£200; witches £40-£60.

Boats – Virtuous, New Dawn, Celestial Dawn, Arcana

Peterhead, 9 boats, 2 consignments, landed 3,205 boxes. Monkfish £2.20-£3.40; witches £1-£2 each.

Boats – Lapwing, Budding Rose, Harvest Hope, Fruitful Bough, Fair Morn

I like the story I once heard of William Stafford. He said his habit was to write a poem every day. When asked how he managed to write so much, he thought a moment and answered "Some days I lower my standards." The story may be true, is possibly apocryphal, but comes to mind writing this journal. I have too many words. What's written here is spontaneous, I've nothing to lose but the words. It may be a broadcloth journal, from cutout bits from poems; the poems are the holes in the cloth from which they've been cut. Like the Jain image of the released spirit, a negative, since they're not yet written. In the surrounding material are many repetitions in the pattern, like speech. What goes down here is only words. Attributed to Allen Ginsberg, (but certainly first articulated by Chogyam Trungpa, the Tibetan refugee who co-founded Samye Ling Tibetan Centre in Eskdalemuir) on spontaneity: First thoughts, best thoughts. If I think anything it's probably: Having thoughts? Think again.

All words. I'm having a clear-out, there's too many for my storage space. I've an incomplete set of oddities if anyone would like them, previously enjoyed (as car-salesmen say): unguent and ungulate. Some are words related to religion that I really should bin, like zealot and apocrypha, but they can be sold these days to newspapers. I have trouble getting out the word aspen, also, nearly always saying poplar instead. I blame Linnaeus. The botanic name of aspen is Populus tremula: the trembling poplar. I left a poplar for an aspen elsewhere in this journal. If you find it, it's yours.

11th

There's a solitary wood ant roaming the colony at the road bend. At the colony on the rock above this, yet more has slid to the rock below, but that landslide, that cityslide, seems abandoned. There's not a sign of the multitude of webs of a couple of mornings ago. We're all stunned by last night's heavy rain. The geometric webs are made by spiders of the Araneidae family. A study on Islay by the Biology Department of the then Paisley College, of Peatland Spider Communities, may reveal, of the 24 spiders listed, that some are orbweavers, like those here. I cannot tell. I scan their names but all that's revealed is the beauty of another language naming: *Pardosa pullata*, *Alepecosa pulverulenta*, *Centromerita concinna*, *Lepthyphantes zimmermanni* and *Lepthyphantes mengei*; the boldly named *Pirata piraticus*, the posing *Antista elegans* and *Silommetapus elegans*, and *Oedothorax gibbosus*. Some of these are the builders of the hammock webs I saw: money spiders to us. And for sure, they represent the riches of earth and the Earth. Orbweavers, money spiders, wolf spiders, together with other small fauna leading their stamped on and hidden lives, and with gastropods, literally bind the fabric of the earth together. It's because of these small and slow creatures that I see each trunk a habitat, each stand of bracken or bog-myrtle a copse; a map of someone's territory.

16th

Andromeda galaxy, 300 billion stars' light taking 2 million years to reach us, cold. At 21.09 tonight, stags are belling through rut and, above the mountain's faint horizon, through the air-splitting roar of a low flying fighter jet leaving only its faster-than-sound anger. At 21.11 the jet returns, a little north. And passes round again at 21.15. There's a rustling in the dying bracken.

17th

the small rural
newspaper soon
read through

Ozaki Hosai (whose poem that is, in translation by William J Higginson), the early-twentieth-century Japanese poet, led a troubled and alcoholic life. Perhaps his drinking arose from the fact that he was not allowed to marry the woman he loved, as she was too close a relative. He worked in insurance for many years, before becoming a Buddhist monk at Shodoshima (small-bean-island). A colleague in insurance described him as reeking of alcohol early in the morning. Although fellow workers wore business suits, Hosai owned no clothes except a pair of pyjamas and a tuxedo, which is what he wore to work.

the nail box:
every nail
is bent

Hosai was a chronicler of the overlooked. Just outside the door here, next to the roll of waiting-to-be-used sheep fencing, is a handleless feed bucket full of nails. Each one is rusty and as unusable as bent nails (though in years gone by I've straightened and reused many a pulled nail).

De tha dol?, too, our small newspaper here is very soon read through, scanned eagerly for news of distant neighbours, notices of any change in shop opening hours or a fund-raising event. Though we go back to it the following day, for fear of having missed something. A sheep dog trial is a big event here, where we really do leave our doors open. Who'd come in but neighbours? There are no burglars, where even a visitor's straying dog is seen a mile away by more than one pair of eyes. As I recall, there's only been one theft recorded in De tha dol? in recent months – back in May, a sundial was taken from a garden in Ardnastaing and featured in the Letters Page. Neighbours come and go, entering houses at will, to leave mail given them by the postman for safe delivery. Once, here, my neighbour came in while I was away at the ferry. She was in need of a drink, but since I was not in, took a bottle and glass and had a drink at the table. Then, when I wasn't soon back, wandered off with the bottle. I took this as a compliment. She knew me well enough to know I'd have happily joined her in a drink and sent her away with a bottle; if she'd appeared next morning in a tuxedo, we'd both have known that's how life gets. I've carried small poems of Hosai's in my head for more than thirty years, the way sheds and porches carry tins and boxes of bent nails and torn-slotted screws. It's proof, as if needed, that poetry, when rooted in the personal, the closely observed, moves far beyond the cultural grounding of its origin and becomes culture.

*at midnight
a distant door
pulled shut*

20th

Port round up:

Mallaig: Progress fishing the Minch, Wanderer III fishing the Firth of Clyde.
Buckie: Boats: Achieve, Aspire, Pegasus, Loyal Friend, Illustrious, Vigilant, Osprey, Silver Rock.
Pelagic vessel landings and nephrops at Mallaig and Peterhead. Witches all over.

26th

It's been a long time since anyone called me son, but the old woman was surely entitled to do that according to age. It's certainly a splendid thing to be called son by someone who's not my parent. It reminds of a time (maybe imaginary) when the elderly were seen as wise in the ways of the world; when an old woman could respectfully be called cailleach. The term has overtones also of nun and of a childless woman. This makes it all the more endearing – a real human exchange is made in the one casual word. It's full of genuine humanity, a trust that's often far from us, with our care for our own narrow self-interest and that of our immediate circle. When we discriminate against those who are not "our" children, it's possible to close an eye to other children's suffering. Pick up a magazine to see how we objectify the starving, maiming and sexualisation of others' children, scarcely able to part ourselves from the SUV which takes "our" kids to school.

Vandana Shiva, the physicist and eco-activist wrote that we go to the woods to learn democracy. (I paraphrase from memory). In these woods here, is a co-dependent community of trees. That community is symbiotic with all the other communities, the microflora, the flora – from orchids to lichens – each with its contribution to the general woodland structure; the fauna and small creatures that I've already written of here in the journal: wood-ants, spiders, slugs, along with the beetles and wasps and flies. I have no idea how many species there are in these woods, never mind individuals of each species: the number is incalculable. Yet here is true democracy, with all these creatures having the right to exist (unless tampered with by a landowner who sees them as subject to his whims and economic will) in and of themselves, valued (is that too strong a word? I think not where absence of one leads to the degradation of the whole) equally for their contribution. Our recently elected government wants a conversation with Scotland. If it were to extend that conversation to the commons – the woodlands, the heaths and bogs, mosses and mires; to the voiceless, then we might all begin to live deliberately. The curlew at dusk has more resonance than the bleatings of parliaments; the small sound of a dragonfly laying its eggs in a sidestream, the tok tok of a stonechat, and the kind word of an old woman. It's not so much that we don't value the trees and their fellows, we simply don't see them. What we see is largely economic. What price can we derive from timber. Of course there's an increasingly recreational attitude: what fun can I have in a woodland, as well as the neo-sacred and neo-mystic: how do the trees enhance my personal growth and healing (and nurture my delusions). We seldom allow woods to be for their own sake; that would be to admit that we're all on an equal footing, co-existing in a fragile and complex space. There are no meetings with remarkable trees – all trees and therefore all woods, are remarkable. The Sunart oakwoods are also remarkable in their survival of economic appropriation. I'd like to see them survive for their own sake; not simply because they're a place of quiet vitality in a busy world – they're part of that same world – and can refresh busy people and inject a little calm into folks' lives (which they do), but because they have as much right to exist as we do.

Meanwhile, here at Ard Airigh, I've been soaked twice and dried twice walking through the woods today. I've tried to step on as few plants as possible, but they're forgiving, my tread only marginally heavier than that of a hind. Glimpses of the loch through the trees and the occasional sun shafts releasing the last delicate flies from where they shelter, and I'm still carrying the old woman piggyback in my mind.

28th

Two days' heavy rain, driven by westerlies, and the burns overspill and topple white and fast down the hills. The bare rock faces gleam in lulls and rainbows flash on and off as the sun and rain chase across the

heights, mostly north, sometime south. The ant colony nearest is sodden and quiet. I suppose the ants to be in hibernation. In what way they hibernate, Maeterlinck's *The Life of the Ant* does not recount. It's my ant bible; though it's stuffed as full of myth, suppositions, parallels, wishful thinking and righteousness as the Christian bible, it has an easy story-telling and at times, elegant prose. Maeterlinck only writes of the ant at rest:

"When after a long adventure, burdened with booty three or four times her own weight, she returns to the nest, her companions who guard the entries hasten to meet her and… cleanse her of the dust that covers her, brushing and caressing her, and lead her to a sort of sleeping-chamber, far from the tumult of the crowd, which is reserved for exhausted travellers. There she soon sinks into a slumber…".

I had visualised ants hugger-mugger together, like sleeping puppies; hibernating like dormice or the hedgehog who lives the winter out under my raised wooden hut at Carbeth. But I'm sure this is not the case. In fact the colony gives every appearance of being deserted; wet through, there must be a drainage system inbuilt, just as there are ventilation ducts in the architecture. But to see the mushroom growing from one side is to doubt this. It may be Bolbitius vitellinus, it may not and seeing it, I'm reminded of the moss creeping once more onto the cold roofs of holiday and second home cottages now the fires remain unlit in ashy hearths. Wet again, the hound and I return, she to crunch her bone and sprawl across the floor (she's the best part of five feet from nose to tail tip and uses a lot of space) and my glass fills as I listen to rain hard on the window and peel yellowed birch leaves from my boots.

29th

The landscape of my childhood was littered with snapped and chewed pencils, the wooden pencil being a necessary tool for turning wayward boys into scholars, as was the birch, according to the then prevalent educational theories, or at any rate practices. In all the little inlets of the loch, where the land descends in the grip of rock to the edge of the water grow those great colonisers, birches. Many, having seeded themselves in the most exposed places and grown to a certain age have snapped at the leading edge, leaving only a broken and chewed looking stub. They grow in fours, fives and sixes. Maybe one is weaker than the others, or closer to prevailing gales and storm weather and snaps. This leaves a wind passage, for they all draw a little shelter from each other, and one by one, the others crack, being brittle rather than sinewy enough to bend with the wind. The weight of leaves and twigs will fold the tree top down, where it becomes a titbit for any passing deer. Those that survive, if it were not for the deer and sheep grazing seedlings and in lean winters eating the bark, shelter other species of tree. They act as nurses to alders, oak, rowan, holly. If there were no sheep and no human interference, there would be good woodland regeneration in a short space of time.

I like to think of pencils made of birch wood, but I know that most are made from cedar, a few, still, from pine. In Tibet ten years ago, I would sit down wherever I could to rest from the thin air and write with my pencil – the only thing it's possible to write with in the rain. Everywhere a shy child would appear at my elbow, even where I could see no houses. The girl, or sometimes boy, would look at my pencil, look at my paper and look at me. I let her write, or sometimes the very young would draw. The pencil would be reluctantly handed back. When I stood, I would make a small gift of the pencil. We can get pencils cheap. China sells them by the million. When I need a pencil now, I wander along the streets that Scottish schoolchildren use and find them littering the ground, unchewed, seldom broken.

The pencils may not be made of birch, but from Sailean nan Cuileag just over the hill, the last loads of birch brooms were taken away at the end of the last century. The brooms were used in the Clydeside steel foundries. They were made in dark winter, as piece work at 4½ d a dozen, less than 2p. Hugh Cameron claimed to Alastair Cameron to be able to make 24 dozen in nine hours, which included felling the trees. Timber was shipped from the little bays and inlets around here for centuries, Sailean nan Cuileag, Port na h-Uamha, Camusaine, (where the number of trees was recorded precisely, as 41,070) for building, for charcoal, bark-oak for tanning. Cameron, again, records "all the tree except the crash it made when falling was used". In the 1870s fellers and snedders were paid 16 shillings a week, a high wage in comparison to the birch-broom makers. Lost trades go with lost language and their gear and tackle. For tanning, the bark was taken from the bottom of the tree before it was felled. In Gaelic this was called moganachadha, and was a skilled job in itself. The moss was scraped off with a *sgrioban coinnich* which was curved to fit the tree; smaller branches were peeled – *spitheagadh* – by girls. I've yet to discover any Gaelic speaker here who knows these terms who did not come across them as I did, in Cameron's Annals, written within living memory.

Peeled branches, as well as pencils also littered my childhood, but then I didn't have to peel them to earn a crust.

31st

Five days after full moon and still there's light through torn clouds greater than the starlight, looming Ben Resipole at the end of the road I'm walking. No lights but for these. All the steading lights are out across the bay; the stags are no longer moaning in Moidart or Laga. Late curlews waver their calls across the leaden sea at Eilean Dubh. The cold bites the bridge of my nose and I'm suddenly and unassailably happy and singing: the sign painted on the road bend is SLOW and oh I don't hurry; I step slowly into the night's mysteries and out across the turf under which a million infinitesimally small creatures lead their lives in the forever dark, through which owls and bats swoop thick and noiselessly and the slugs slowly curve their way. Fresh rain drops on my hatless head; my neighbours the mountains dream on.

November
3rd

It's the old way, still the way of most of the world, but it's become remote and we try to banish it: to walk unaided by light in darkness. How apart and rare. Now ten days after full moon, four until a new moon. No houselights east or west. A little dim starlight as the west wind frays the lumbering mass of greyed cloud. To slowly feel the way with cautious feet. To feel alone in silence. To feel cold in dim mountain bulk, the absence of complication, world reduced to the slow and slowing unseen but present; like the presence of the liver and spleen in the body – unfelt but known of. Stags in the dark. Birds roosted. One step. And another.

5th

In Scandinavia, the burning of birch has led to whole technologies of the wood-burning stove. Although it gives off a good heat, it's no sooner lit than burned through. There's plenty of it here, as in Scandinavia, but here also we have oak, the quintessential firewood, lasting long and burning hot. Firewood has been taken from these woods as long as people and woods have co-existed here, with folk still taking logs and brushwood, though nowadays most wood, if felled and if removed (rather than left for the slow energy burn of beetles, wasps and spiders and their kin) goes for other purposes. In other times, holly was said to burn like wax; plenty of ash was laid to a fire, burning as it does green or seasoned. I still start fires when I can with knuckles of ash, from faggots collected under the trees when storms crack off limbs and shower down twigs. Likewise the whitethorn, which burns hot and is said to bake the best bread. Rowan also burns hot, but though I've saved the trunk and arms of a storm-felled rowan for three seasons, I'm too superstitious to burn it; rowans guard a house, and although I sometimes believe this and sometimes don't, it's just not polite to burn your guardians.

The bonfire to celebrate Guy Fawkes (though there was no effigy of himself or the Pope) was a huge wigwam of scrap wood on the foreshore at Salen. I've no idea what types of wood it was made up of; though it's a fair bet that most of it came from elsewhere. As far as I could tell, it was salvaged from demolitions and renovations of local houses; though there appeared to be the sides of an old shed, entire. It felt mean at a fine public festivity, of which there are too few left, to be thinking of the use all that wood could be put to. When the man from Salen said, almost in a whisper, that it was a shame to see all that heat wasted, I couldn't but agree. But; and but, the anarchist, the peasant at the tumbrel, the child in me, was overjoyed to see the fire catch and take in the offshore wind, flames neither dancing nor licking, but drinking the wood. It was the sparks that danced in that elemental dance, retaining the shape of the hot updraughts, pushed this way and that like stars at the beginnings of time; that same dance of purest elation, driven by the same force, to be seen in shoaling fish and swarming bees and the swoop of starlings at dusk as they prepare to roost and pour into a tree or ivied wall.

It all made a fitting spree for the passing into winter, although it was past All Saints and All Souls Days. The flames, if you believe such things, may have helped souls of the faithful attain their places elsewhere. Saints needed no such help, having probably already been roasted to ensure their sojourn in the clouds. With harps. (or is that angels?) Myths are fun, and the month is called Samhain in Gaelic anyway, meaning harvest and surely a time to remember the dead and that we're alive and with a fine crop.

The commemoration of a man who didn't succeed in blowing a parliament to hell and which led to excesses of anti-Catholicism (why do

I think of the Revd. Paisley and his refined sense of smell: "No pot-pourri here!"); the celebration of Halloween, itself a kind of Christian theft of the harvest hullabaloo of Samhain, at which cattle bones were thrown in fires to ensure prosperity for the coming year (indeed the word bonfire or bonefire is said by some to be a direct translation of the Gaelic tine cnamh), all makes for a mix where, like at the edges of the fire, at this fringe of the Sunart oakwoods, distinctions become blurred. Perhaps the more so because it's damned cold and we're outside the pub clutching our whisky glasses, but within sight of the still crackling blaze on the shore and its sense of redemption for those damned in the myths. Though I note that over the road the big house was once a Temperance Hotel, so maybe the whisky will lead us all to perdition. Or to laughter: the same place for an unbeliever.

The children, tumbling in the wet, leaping from the walls, clattering into shins and yelling, are there already.

My prevailing sense of anarchy, the child in me at this bonfire, has echoes in an unpublished chronicle I'm privileged to read – *A Highland Boyhood in Ardnamurchan*, written by Angus Cameron, who grew up here and like most of his generation in the peninsula, had no English before he went to school. It was loaned to me by my neighbour, a cousin of his, but even though she and one of her sisters and another relative try to unravel the knot of kinship, it remains tied and unresolved as to what degree of cousin. He writes of Kentra in the years of the First World War: "As the year rolled round, Hallowe'en was looked forward to with great fervour, as a crowd of us would dress up to go out "guising" and get involved in a host of pranks and tricks. Boats and carts would be removed and replaced in somebody else's croft or patch. The shoemaker (Allan) guarded his boat carefully, but as soon as he left for a cup of tea, we would have it shifted. One year we put it beside John George's potato pit, exchanging it with John George's cart, which we left on the shore."

6th

Smoke's curling out from the top of the chimney; the day is grey, a shade somewhere between the meditating heron's back and the negative-blackness of the cormorants barely skimming the salt water. The light begins to fail at four o' clock on November days like this and a prolonged dusk adds to the sombreness of the day. Sea in the bay reflects nothing.

There's no break in cloud cover, only layerings of darker and dark. I'm taken by surprise, then, by the vivid yellow of the furze bushes to the west of the bay. As I warm my eyes with their glow, I'm distracted by the dartings of a wren, brown in her cave of spikes. Sheep graze furze in hard winters; I'm thinking it would need to be hard indeed to get past those inch long spines, which are in fact its leaves. It was once ground as cattle fodder and is still fed to horses who apparently delight in it. I'm lost in the quick jinking of the wren and the hardiness of this plant, when the rich almond smell of the flowers reaches my nose; it's zesty and sends me straight back to childhood kitchens and marzipan. Warmed by memory, scent and sight, I stroll on, nonchalant in the cold wind.

7th

The wind's blowing up from the west again and from the point above the ants that looks out over Eilean Dubh I can see ocean spume. Although the ants are in full hibernation, beside their small dwelling I find a pair of Scarlet Hoods. These mushrooms are blood red with a waxy feel and shine among dead bracken and deep-sea green moss. They're also edible, so into my hat they go for safe passage home. Then, with the easy optimism of an early find, the hound and I set off mushrooming in the woods.

The woods, like me, are not sure if autumn is coming or going. The oaks are browning and crisping their leaves, one tree at a time. It's not age, nor yet exposure that causes this patchwork undressing, but perhaps an expression of health or of individuality, with here a mature tree in green leaf, there a partially clad elder and here a stripped fifty year old youngster. The taller hollies are vibrant with berries, a signifier of a bad winter, it's said. Other hollies here seem close cropped, perhaps by deer; certainly they're very low and appear to be layering into small groves, but no taller than mid calf. They have no berries, so maybe they are too young, or simply all male trees. The willows are still leaved. The Scots pines are direct from a Chinese mountains and waters landscape scroll, with their backdrop of soft-toothed hills. A signature is the final spindly foxglove, with its single purple bell.

It's a joy to walk in these damp, duff-smelling moss clad woods; I think of Sweeney, exiled, mad, and his naked wanderings in the woods of Ireland and Britain: "Dense wood is my security, / the ivy has no edge." in Trevor Joyce's perfect translation. and "I occupy in alien woods / an old retreat; / in my familiar square of trees / shrewd centre of such intimate quincunx am I". Quincunx, where he counts himself a tree. Indeed, it's so silent here, that the slight sibilance of our exhalation is equal to the fall of sap in these oaks.

Of mushrooms, though, not a smell; save for a single psilocybe. I stravaig north and west; past the trunk where once was frosted chicken-of-the-woods, a dim memory in the skillet now, past the small stand of beech and deeper into the oaks, where, still serving my stomach, I take the consolation of a bite of wood sorrel (Sweeney: "Though you relish salted hams / and the fresh meat of ale-houses, / I would rather taste a spray of cress / in some zone exempt from grief.") But the truth is, the sorrel's tough and at the uttermost end of its season.

Once, I would have been pleased by the psilocybe, but with deep woods and scarlet hoods singing bloodred in my brain, now they stay unplucked. Hinds and stags have no such scruples, browsing through the woods. Nor the slugs. What does a slug experience, nibbling on Russula emetica: the Sickener? Hard to imagine a slug with vertigo, or seeing flashing lights, or even vomiting. These are the toxic effects on humans of this little cherry coloured mushroom. Fly agaric seems to be eaten with impunity by deer. It has, of course been taken for its psychotropic qualities over the ages in northern woods. I've eaten it raw and any psychotropic experience – the flashing lights, organic curlicues of Green-Mannishness and an overwhelming certitude (of what, is never asked) – is second only to uncontrollable shivering and prodigious, endless vomiting. Americans also assert, helpfully, "it fries the liver". It has also been taken when passed through another's liver. Some stories have it the liver of a deer, others the livers of the rich, (poor people being unable to afford the mushroom: but this doesn't stand scrutiny, much; poor people need only go to the woods. But again, parenthetically, we might ask what else have the rich ever done for the piss-poor). Mrs Beeton might say: first catch your deer. and what would the rooted and branched stags experience in the way of apparition and delusion from psychotropic agarics? Safely through a liver, then, the urine may be drunk: result – intoxication without toxicity. I've met men who've drunk turps and even brasso and achieved a kind of Sweeney-state; they'd maybe drink urine too, if they were half the believers that our current ranks of neo-shamans and Latter Day Druids are. Sweeney was never half so deluded.

The hound looks at me – I've sat still long enough. All day, we've seen nothing moving but a wren; heard nothing but the running water of burns among boulders thick with moss, and now the lowing of cattle over the hill towards Polloch. It's just two Scarlet Hoods then, with my supper eggs and potato. At the kitchen table, I'm eating and leafing through Dogen's "Instructions to the Cook": ("When you prepare food, never view the ingredients from some commonly held perspective, nor think about them only with your emotions.") and out flutters a small clipping. It's dated by me in pencil 12 11 05, almost precisely two years old. It's from *The Guardian*, and in entirety reads: "Swedish papers reported the tale of the rampaging, drunken elks that threatened to attack an old people's home. The old people were saved, but the elks were following well-documented behaviour that included attacks on joggers and cyclists after feasting on fermented apples."

8th

A gale here and stronger wet squalls coming with northwesterlies. Rain's dashed down against the slates but the strength of wind curling round Gobsheallach hill contrariwise pushes it upwards again to sing over the roof ridges. Rain takes turns with bouncing hail. The hound is unnerved by the squalls; facing them the air is forced into her long nose and sets her sneezing, behind and she's forever looking over her shoulder to see what the noise back there is bringing. In a sheltery dip she puts up a sudden snipe from the bracken where neither of us saw it until it flew a few feet. It slid sideways in the wind and curved up slightly, in that deceptive way of snipe, before, blown, clipping a small birch trunk and then running into the heather and over the rock; more pheasant than snipe. She may be sheltering or may have been pushed down by the gale and injured a wing. If that's the case, it's the fox who'll benefit tonight.

It won't be the same fox, but the story is told of the fox trotting down the hillside here and along the road past the house over by. The man of the house sees the fox, bold as brass, and fearing for the hens, runs inside for maybe a gun, but comes out with only a hearth brush, which he lobs anyway at the fox. The fox, nonchalant, turns, throws a look, grabs the brush in his smirking teeth and trots on his way. When the farm is having a new shed built, two-three years later, a fallen trunk needs to be moved; in a den underneath, dry and in good condition is the red hearth brush. I think it's in use to this day.

9th

SHIPPING NEWS

A maritime seasonal gauge at Ardtoe Jetty is the number of boats at moorings. In the summer there's a dozen or more small boats, a couple of which are working boats, bringing home in an infrequent way, lobsters and crabs. These boats, mostly pleasure craft, are brought ashore, one at a time, as the oak and aspen leaves fall around them. Today, there's only three boats and two RIBs. The RIBs act as tenders to the two small fishing boats, OB 108 being one, and will ride the winter here. The only boat I've seen there with a name, Tarbaby, has gone.

Caledonian MacBrayne ferries from Mallaig to Eigg, Rum, Muck and Canna did not operate yesterday in the storms and squally winds.

Among the boats from Fraserburgh and Peterhead that put out: Valhalla, Tranquility, Ocean Pioneer, Contest, Courage, Accord, Achieve, Celestial Dawn, Arcane, Fear Not, Opportunus, Harvest Hope, Challenge, Fruitful Bough. One boat put out from Scrabster: Seagull.

Monks and witches landed everywhere.

11th

*– through metaphor to reconcile
the people and the stones.*

Thinking about William Carlos Williams' short poem 'A sort of a song'. That reconciliation is difficult, even when I know there's no real separation, no such thing as independent existence. It's what Dogen meant when he wrote of mountains constantly walking. The bedrock does not protrude from the mosses, it wears them. The trees don't displace air and water, but contain them.

The night of the new moon and the rain has not let up any, coming in hard twisting ribbons curling across the woodland. In a search for shelter, or maybe just restless, frogs leap high across the road. A sullen elk-wet stag, shaggy and hunched, steps out from my torchlight and behind the dripping oak at Camas a Choirce.

The following day in Morvern, by Laudale, the wind persists, buffeting until the shelter of the trees at Aird Beitheach, the high birches, is reached. Leaves swoop back into these trees with the wind, dipping from tree to tree, up at the last moment to land on the topmost twigs, to resolve themselves into a flock of tits and treecreepers, momentarily leafing the bare birch and oak in their own fashion. At night small mammals are constantly running across the road, perhaps mice or voles, tawny brown and rushing from one side to the other before revealing their nature as dried leaves scuttering in wind.

Then, last night, pulled from the trees, the last downtwisting small birch leaves, despite the intense cold, become what they maybe were all along: flimsy breezy moths. There's a brown owl sitting on the fence, fully awake, and I guess tired of moths.

*(No ideas
but in things)*

Williams wrote in the same poem. Things have their own ideas, they're themselves, sometimes idea-less, happening, an event, walking their own way.

13th

Is a stag an event? There's no wind, droplets of water on every aspen, birch and oak, as well as at the tip of each stalk of hard rush. Ambling across the bay west from Kentra, two hours ahead of low tide, pausing only to scratch, the dark necked stag owns it all. I move up the hill to cut him off and sit quietly where he'll come ashore. To see things, it's easier to be still than to lumber behind. I sit for maybe twenty minutes until the damp seeps in. Experience says he's scented me and moved off below or above. There's no further sight of him.

In the afternoon I walk round the headlands on the bay's sands and there's his slotted hoofprints leading in to an inlet east of where I was sitting in the morning. It's among the poised and ponderous heron prints, each foot just about the span of my hand. The ridges and wrinkles of the bay are crisscrossed by worm casts and the meanderings of small whelk trails and the musings of other shellfish creeping. Just as the outlines of heron, stag and fish prints are softening in the moisture retained in the sand's striations, so are the lower slopes of watercut hills of rock around the bay blurring into cloud; the peak of Ben Resipole rising into sun. The stag's away.

15th

> *swords into ploughshares*
> *spears into grafting knives*

> *a gunmetal sea*

and when I write grey skies I think of Gertrude Stein. These are not grey skies but curling greyladen clouds, formless in wisps and solids, changing their formlessness as wind drives them. Light and dark according to density, the load of moisture they hold, that they are. Nothing recognisable, as different from yesterday's grey sky as the shapes clouds don't become. No trees, faces, monsters. They're all down here, where here is. All morning behind that grey a reverberance above cloud tops; another unseen jet rolling over the sky, rumbling the hills here. I'd thought the manoeuvres and ravening aerobatic displays over, that air force jets had ended, another seasonal event, going into underground hangars like the wood-ants, to sleep and dream of becoming. But this is probably a last summer visitor who can't wait to catch his fellows in their fall migration to the middle east, the mountains of Afghanistan and plains of Iraq

17th

> *sleet or snow?*
> *feels good it soaks into.*
> *my body wet.*
> *mistily moistened.*
> *snow or cold rain?*
> *acanthus rooting above me gone bad for the cold?*
> *or those withered leaves suffering heavy snow?*
> *what's that faint sound coming on?*
> *a jet?*

I find it hard to observe frogs closely without being distracted by fragments of Kusano Shimpei's poems. That one is from *monologue of a hibernating frog* (translated from the Japanese by Cid Corman with Susumu Kamaike) and it's what frogs should be doing round about now, not leppin across roads in front of cars and pickups and heavy boots. But there they are.

Making sure they don't dry out; though in Sunart oakwoods, it's just about impossible to dry out. There's no doubt though that the year is somewhat warmer for longer than is usual. Over on the north shore of Loch Sunart, close by the wrecks of two small boats, ragged robin, *Lychnis flos-cuculi*, is still in flower. Here at Gobsheallach, right outside the door are the tall purple flowers and foliage of spear thistle, *Cirsium vulgare*; up the hill, as elsewhere around, male catkins of hazel share a branchlet with as yet unshed and now lime-green autumn leaves. I mention this in the bliss of ignorance. The thistle and ragged robin are summer flowering, yet here we are in mid November. How easy to use phrases like global warming; the truth is, there are complex factors at work here, which such easiness undermines. It's certainly the case that plants have a wider period of flowering than memory or text books generally allow. Frogs make up their own minds, according to temperature. And Kusano. And here we are in a temperate zone (and therefore basically not too extreme), in what amounts to a rainforest, made so partly by the north Atlantic drift. Frogs may come and go as they please, to a certain extent, using the glucose in their blood as a kind of anti-freeze; though I grant, not of their own volition. When they do hibernate, it's in a hibernaculum. What a grand word for sleeping in mud.

But neither the frogs nor myself are sleeping the winter away yet. There's a half-moon, lying on its back among broken clouds, the way I feel to be, looking up at the few visible stars, but no sign of the Leonid meteors, which are only for three days from the 16th to the 18th of this month; nor of the shooting stars that my star chart predicts. Peter tells me also that I might be able to see the comet Holmes, in Perseus, not too far (though that has to be relative) from Andromeda.

I see only the frogs tonight

proceeding quietly single file.
long silent single file.
file of frogs proceeding.

from *Lululu's funeral (accompanied by Chopin's funeral march)* Kusano Shimpei.

19th

I can feel the frost coming. The air is cold and still. Chimney smoke over by Kentra, not moved by any wind, drops to the bracken and rolls, spreading like liquid. The sky has cleared itself of sulky grey and the moon has already risen high. There are two sunsets this evening. One, the colour of an angry boil against a few delicate stratus clouds slips behind Torr Beithe, the tor of beeches, now conifers. The other, the colour of salmon flesh is hard against me in the sea by Eilean Dubh. A curlew's thin thread of a call as she rises stitches the two.

With the moon nearly full, the shadow of the two rowans just by here and my own shadow as I pass by them are as distinct as any negative formed by the sun. There are no Leonids, comets or shooting stars; the moon is enough, picking out the shine of rock. This moon is the Blood Moon, it's written on my almanac, with vague neopagan overtones.

20th

There is a second flush of growth in oak and other trees, known as lammas growth. It happens in the summer and is a response to temperature and other factors favourable to a fresh surge of growth. The tree is most prone to this when it's young; it doesn't happen in old trees. Nicolas Battey, writing in the *Journal of Experimental Botany*: "This decline could be conceived as learning from experience… A youthful tree shows lammas growth. It seems an enthusiasm, an impetuous response to summer warmth and light. With age, it declines, and the tree settles down to more sedate growth." It's a kind of freedom of expressive growth; it's not the expansion of spring laid down the previous year. I don't doubt that trees also learn from experience; to see any tree in Sunart oakwoods reacting, however slowly, to prevailing wind and the falling of old limbs from gales and lightning is to see trees balancing on rocky slopes in a decades long dance.

Lammas Day, August 1st, ("so call'd from the Mass said for preservation of Lambs") is perhaps a Christian pilfering of Lughnasadh, the festival to celebrate the start of the harvest season, the growth that has given the first fruit.

It may be there is a correlative to trees' lammas growth in the ragged robin and the spear thistle; a learning and an urge to make a fresh spurt, an utterance of life. An impetuous response. A song.

Also with a new burst of expansion are the jet planes, which have not yet made their eastward migration, but were only waiting on fine weather to make their high-sky vapour hieroglyphs, which fade to parentheses and the symbol for eternity; a figure eight on its side. These offensive jets (I'm using the MoD term) are Harriers and Tornadoes. Somewhere between the swept back wings of Tornadoes are Storm Shadow and Brimstone missiles, as well as General Purpose Bombs and Cluster Bombs which sow their submunitions over a couple of acres to flower at will. In other fields. Some of these aircraft rip to Ardnamurchan from Lossiemouth, about 150 miles as the crow flies. The vapour symbols are probably scrawled by a defensive Typhoon; the Eurofighter.

Among the boats returning to land fish today are: New Dawn, Celestial Dawn, Fruitful Vine, Fruitful Harvest, Harvest Hope and Ocean Harvest.

23rd

At sunrise, together with a hind limned against a lightening sky, I watch as the bay becomes gold across its newborn sand. The news bulletin told me of Palestinians waking to the bulldozing of precious and ancient olive trees uprooted to make way for the concrete wall. The sun gilding sand is heart stopping, an organ played on by the blood of hind and human.

The hind moves on delicate black hooves over rock and heather, downhill, elegantly scratching her ear with her right rear leg; maybe, now in calf, she's in as contemplative a mood as myself. I move up hill in a sky rapidly silvering then greying as the sun rises above the bay, above Ben Resipole's hip and above rain clouds moving in from the Atlantic. The birches and the moss below are full of the flit and dart of chaffinches. The males echo the day, with their blue-grey crowns and rosy breasts, with the upcoming generation, or so I take it to be, slightly less coloured, but they'll grow into it. The female is altogether olive brown. A grey crow, one of a pair in an alder, is wiping his beak on a branch, with a knife-sharpening motion, to take off traces of breakfast.

Under alder and birch and oak alike, the skeletal remains of bracken keel and reveal the green vividness of sphagnums and the herringbone pattern and green corduroy of shield ferns, (*Polystichum aculeatum* is my stab in the darkness of my own uncertainty). In the oaks grow polypody – *Polypodium interjectum*, their green multiple tongues dripping and refreshingly free of cant.

Dusk comes a little earlier each night, bringing greater safety, but greater hunger to the deer. The Glen Tarbert stags are down from the tops; three of them that I see have almost identical broken left antlers. They're young and their rivalries are over, leaving only those cracked anti-trophies of male hormone flow, subsided as tide in the inlets. At Camas a' Choirce, a solitary fossicking badger trots and snuffles between pounding rain squalls, light on her feet, her belly low-slung and her body-mass-index enough to frighten humans. Mostly nocturnal, she (I have no way of telling the sex of this animal) will spend more time sleeping in the longer colder nights, but have no food shortages just yet; the woods an autumn larder of roots, worms, carrion and mushrooms. At Kentra, young hind calves trot ahead of me, bemused by my torchlight in the pre-moon dark.

Clarity arrives with the full moon. Although there are clouds, the light is brilliant, lighting the white of sheep up on Gobsheallach hillside with a shining matched only by the luminescence of lichen rings on the rocks I finger as personal touchstones as I pass. Scale is confused in such clarity where I find it hard to ascribe anything but equal value to what is in front of my eyes wherever my glance falls – a lunar illumination scaled to fit human perception.

24th

By Castle Tioram the fat handfed black pheasants are strident in their protest at the mere sight of the hound and myself. The dithering birds protest at the hound, who, since they're behind a wire fence, affects not to notice them.

A red squirrel climbs the Scots pine anti-clockwise, finding tiny things of interest there; its incurved tail meagre and rufous. It cares as little for all of us as the hound for the pheasants, as I do for the man who pays the breeder of the birds, reared only to be killed; food a long way from consideration.

The hound makes a hiccupping sally towards a rabbit on the island the castle sits on.

A herring gull mourns overhead.

28th

I seem to inhabit time backwards these quick days; a regression into memory. As a child, I heard of Eskimoes having hundreds of words for snow. Now I know that Franz Boas the anthropologist recorded just four: to mean lying snow, falling snow, drifting snow and snow drift. This, in just one language of the many of the people I now know as Inuit. Maybe there are many more Boas was not told. Here, there's rain. It's falling straight down and is constant. This morning's Shipping Forecast gave six options for rain around the country: occasional rain, rain then showers, rain or showers, continuous moderate rain, slight drizzle and rain, and finally, occasional rain or drizzle. Before going out, I try to decide which I'm seeing through the kitchen window. It must be continuous moderate rain. Fliuch; wet then, in Gaelic. There's no wind. Our words in English for rain – drizzle, showers, heavy rain, squalls, pour into my mind as the moderate rain falls on my green knitted hat.

One of this year's piebald lambs – a cross of a blackface tup with a Hebridean ewe – with one and a half thin horns, nuzzles the hens where they disconsolately scratch the sogged turf. Up the hill water abandons its usual courses across and through thin soil, and being pragmatic, takes to the roads to follow its way to the bay. Which might be fresh rather than salt in all this rain. Fresh now, as though it's the first time I've seen this (though in truth it's an abiding memory from I don't know when), on every hard rush blade, at the junction of each now-dead flowerhead and stem, drops of water catch my eye, rinse my sight.

At the point that looks out to the Atlantic, the morning's heron voices her displeasure at my appearance and cracks long wings over to the island, to the looping, lingering call of her always companion, the curlew.

As the short day eases into dusk, the rain clears and a dilute sun sets a little west of the Tor of Beeches, its off-vermilion blush momentarily lending the hills a purple light among clinging clouds; as though the heather was again flowering as it did in summer. As the small stems of stork's bill, *Erodium cicutarium*, flower unseen and unseasonal, by the sea's edge right here, right now.

29th

Ten in the morning and the waning moon rides high in a wild sky. There's every kind of cloud here, cumulus, black in its lumbering rolling mass, stratus and alto stratus, pulled into ribbons by the wind, all tinged at their edges by the morning sun. The wind pulls tears from my eyes and spreads them across my cold cheekbones. In the bay a cormorant coasts along the gusts, unruffled, a winged lizard, then turns back into the wind for a rising drop into the teeming sea and straight under, wings folded. There's only one mushroom under the birches, a charcoal burner, *Russula cyanoxantha*. Despite its name, this one is good to eat, witness the slight nibbles that a hind has taken. I guess it's a hind since I've seen no stags this way for days. I'm happy to share; I picture it with a breakfast egg, whatever the hind may envisage.

John Cage, an avid mushroom hunter-gatherer, cooker and eater, is not above spreading fallacies concerning mushrooms. In Indeterminacy, he writes "Certain tribes in Siberia trade several sheep for one Amanita muscaria and use the mushroom for orgiastic practices...... The Vikings who went berserk are thought to have done so by means of this same mushroom." The key words here are orgiastic, which goes counter to all the evidence that this was once the intoxicant used during shamans' curative practices; and berserk, for which there is no evidence, though it might perhaps have been a constituent part of an alcohol based cocktail that would send anyone wild; berserk if you will. I'm happy, though that he perpetuates mycophobia, I wonder if it mightn't have been his intention. A mushroom gatherer will do anything to send people away from their patch with the idea that all mushrooms are deadly poisonous. I have several ruses myself. John Cage, again: "Guy Nearing sometimes says that all mushroom experts die from mushroom poisoning. Donald Malcomb finds the dangers of lion hunting largely imaginary, those of mushroom hunting perfectly real." The fact is, though, that mushrooms are one of the last remaining wild foods available here, as elsewhere, and as such belong to those who find them. The law, a notorious ass, and with it the most risible of landowners, would suggest that anything found on a laird's land belongs to him; including wild fruits and fungi. As well then to clear the land of noxious and poisonous mushrooms that I've seen deliberately trampled by those afraid of the orgiastic berserkers who might ingest them. Good with eggs, though, with just a little garlic.

Mushrooms and their association with the woodland here (as everywhere) have a beautiful symmetry. The mycorrhizal connections allow an exchange between tree and fungus of carbohydrates for mineral nutrients which each would find difficult to access otherwise. The exchange is made with a colonisation of the roots of oaks and birch or other trees by fungi. Look for healthy woodland, healthy trees, and they are made so by the fungi which grow on and around them below the soil. Some fungal mycelium mats outlive generations of trees.

Deer nibbling the fruiting bodies – mushrooms – may also bark young trees, but their droppings enrich the woodland floor, making yet more nutrients (droppings derived from their browsing in the Sunart woods) available to tree and mushroom alike. What the Sunart oakwoods may have been like centuries ago, can only be a matter for conjecture. A few years back, the ecologist Frans Vera put forward the theory that's been debated since, that woodland in Europe (and therefore Scotland) was a savannah, with groves and grasses kept open by herds of roaming deer and other mammals. This runs counter to our belief, founded on folklore and perhaps a wish-fulfilment daydream that the ancient woodlands covered Scotland coast to coast in a single continuous closed canopy. Sweeney (*"This clearing is too open, / without trees;..."*) and the Green Man live there.

Whatever the cover of the trees in Sunart's Atlantic oakwoods six thousand years ago and despite being a resource for timber products, the arrival of sheep altered it to such a point that ecologists and conservationists today have difficulties in trying to restore woodlands. I make no secret that I have a fairly low opinion of the intelligence and usefulness of sheep. I'd trade several for a big cep or some chanterelles any day. They were an indirect cause of great suffering (Landlords being the true manipulating culprits) during the Clearances and today have little economic purpose; but I have nothing like the spleen of the good Doctor of Rahoy, John MacLachlan, writing towards the end of the nineteenth century on sheep, shepherds and the subsequent decline of woodland, by then well under way. He writes (in Donald Meek's translation from the Gaelic):

"Alas for my plight here, as I am so lonely,
going through the wood which I once knew closely,
when I cannot get a plot in my native country
though I'd pay a crown for a mere shoe-breadth.

Unsweet is the sound that has roused my reflections,
as it comes down from the heights of Morvern –

> *the Lowland shepherd – how I hate his language! –*
> *bawling yonder to that slow dog of discord.*
>
> *Early on a May morning when it is time to arise,*
> *I hear no music on branches, nor lowing on moorland,*
> *but the screeching of beasts in the English language,*
> *yelling at dogs to make the deer scatter.*
>
> *When I observe the towering mountains,*
> *and the lovely country which was once Fionn's homeland,*
> *I see nothing there but sheep with white fleeces,*
> *and countless Lowlanders at every trysting.*
>
> *The glorious glens where one once found hunting,*
> *where dogs on leashes were held by young fellows,*
> *I see nothing there now but a ragged shepherd,*
> *and his fingers blacker than the crow's pinion.*
>
> *Every old custom has been sent packing – …"*

His poem equates the degradation of the woods with the erosion of language and Gaelic culture, a process that continues to this day. An ecological balance, once unbalanced, must find new purchase on the land: ecology as entropic biodiversity.

December
3rd

I'm woken in the night by squalls of rain syncopating and sloshing on windows and skylights. The sky is black, with rain rushing in on a southwesterly. The morning dawns slowly with no let up in rain; in fact it's becoming fiercer. Wind birls around the byre battering at every window, not just in the prevailing wind direction. The topography here sends the winds into a flurry of indeterminacy, blowing from every quarter, sometimes seemingly at once. It's like dusk all morning. Rain eventually falls away in the early afternoon, but I still don't get too far from the house. Over on the peat bog by Shielbridge, 16 barnacle geese rise reluctantly from the small dug-over sloughs, cackling at my intrusion on their sheltered grazing. They rise as one tattered organism, slowly, peeling heavily into the wind to land a hundred yards away from where I walk, leaning into the wind. Barnacle geese were once believed to come, not from eggs, but from barnacles on the sea shore. Like me, folk learn things through observation; if you've never found a goose nest, because they breed in the Arctic, anything is possible. The shellfish and goose connection is an earlier notion of how things relate: ecology.

From here, looking west, the bulk of Eigg is visible, though not the loom of the Sgurr; there's no sign of Rum behind it. I move back into the wind which the Shipping Forecast had told me is force eight becoming force nine later. I need no forecast to careen into it at a buffeted angle to keep moving forward, just as the geese used the precise and minimal amount of energy to escape my passage. Since the geese are feeding and I'm not, I begin to think of food, (eggs?) with maybe a tot of rum in honour of these two near small islands, surrounded by storms today, and on which doubtless, few geese are moving beyond the next grassy beakful and even fewer people are straying far from the fireplace. A day for a glass of rum in the twilight, window-gazing.

4th

> *My news for you*
> *the stag roars*
> *winter snow*
> *summer is gone*
>
> *wind high and cold*
> *the sun low*
> *quick its course*
> *sea running strong*
>
> *deep-red the bracken*
> *its shape lost*
> *everywhere the cry*
> *of the wild goose*
>
> *frost has hold*
> *of the wings of birds*
> *season of ice*
> *these are my tidings*

Something catches my attention this evening. The wind backs up and blusters somewhere else for the first time in three days. My ears ring in the absence of fast moving air; it's like a reversing truck, how I imagine tinnitus to be. As my ears adjust and begin to stretch my hearing for something else – a curlew maybe; perhaps the hiss of tide retreating –the wind and rain return.

If the anonymous poet of the *Scel lem duib*, (the poem here translated from the Irish with spare elegance by Geoffrey Squires) were to visit Ardnamurchan today and sit here, back to an oak tree in a hollow, watching the tide in the bay, he'd find the land unchanged. Although the stags have now stopped their roar, rutting over, the wind is high and strong and the wild goose frets across the moss. The word *scel* is usually translated as poem or song. Geoffrey Squires, with more than elegance, has the right of it by using the English tidings, and news. It's truly news; a report as fresh this evening as when the poet was first chilled by that wind 1,200 years ago at the end of summer.

Even in my waterproof fleece-lined German ex-army trousers (swords to ploughshares, or at any rate britches) the cold strikes home and I move across the hill into the wind and back to the byre, where the spider is sheltering from the weather.

I'd thought her at first to be a house spider, *Tegenaria saeva* or *domestica*. She's certainly the right size – approaching an inch from eyes to spinner, excluding legs – and moves fast enough; though with a strange patience, if it's that, she'll keep still while I bring the lens to bear on her abdomen and dramatic pedicel. We've been moving around each other from room to room since the southwesterlies first arrived, and by now I'm convinced she's not a house spider, but like any other creature this past week is avoiding rain and the wind that blows rain into cracks and fissures. She has no web that I can find, no cocoon shaped web-dwelling from which to run at prey. Her abdomen is black, as is her carapace, but she lacks any abdominal markings that I can see. I leave her be, both of us in the dry, unfurling bracken days a memory. When I've towelled off, she's nowhere in sight.

5th

The urge toward naming is to make anchors for ourselves in an unreliable mutable world.

The rain's finally stopped, though the wind is as strong as ever. In Antrim last week at a fish farm the entire harvest of salmon, about a hundred and twenty thousand fish was killed, when a mass of mauve stinger jellyfish, Pelagia noctiluca, filled Glenarm Bay. The numbers of mauve stingers was in billions and their mass extended over ten square miles and was thirty-five metres deep. Some salmon died of stings, but most were asphyxiated – the bulk of jellyfish prevented the flow of ocean water into their cages. The high tides and storms probably broke up that swarm, but ocean currents would have sent the jellyfish this way eventually. They have been sighted in the waters around Eigg and in Loch Sunart. Among the boats that work these waters is Speedwell out of Salen on Loch Sunart.

I walk to the fish farm in Ardtoe, from where Eigg, less than an hour's sail from here, can be seen most days. The fish farm is called that still, but is really a hatchery, with its own tanks and waters behind dams away from the shore.

The Bay of Ardtoe, which has no name on the maps, only on the Admiralty Charts, is broad, full of small bays – from Camas an Lighe, the overflowing bay on account of the burn there, where the sands are said to sing in certain conditions, to Sailean Dubh, the black inlet. There's a scattering of skerries – Sgeir an Rathaid, the skerry of the road, Sgeir nam Meann, kid skerry, Dubh Sgeir, Sgeir a' Chaolais.

I stand on the rise above Rubh' a' Mhurain (sea-bent headland). Sea-bent is Arundo arenaria: a grass that, according to Umberto Eco in The Search for the Perfect Language, Linnaeus diagnostically describes as "single flowered within calyx; involute tapering pungent leaves."

I clamber down to the strand. There are no birds in this wind except a pair of cormorants far out toward unseen islands, low, skimming the crests. There is a large belt of kelp washed up to high tide line, but no mauve stingers; in fact Eigg might as well not be there, it can't be seen either, whatever might be swarming in the waters around it. Only a black terrier is moving here, running from one end of the tide-diminished Sailean Dubh to the other at the water line, barking at the incoming ocean. The wind hustles me back onto my heels.

FISH PRICES

Fraserburgh: monk: £70-£80; witches: £30-£60. (per box)
Boats that landed: Guide Us, Ocean Way, Ocean Reaper, Transcend,

Replenish, Concorde, Accord, Gratitude, Serene, Deliverance, Just Reward
Peterhead: monks £2-£3.80; witches 80p-£1.50; megrim £1.50-£4. (each)
Boats that landed: Constant Friend, Ocean Harvest, Our Guide

The names we give out, sometimes at random, to creatures we share space with can sometimes return. The fact that sheep, Ovis aries go by many names, according to gender and age – tup, ewe, lamb, wether, gimmer – doesn't diminish our need to give them personal names. If we get personal names wrong, it's more or less insulting. So a certain tup with one eye, who once inhabited the byre where I now stay, has been offended by my misnaming. I'm happy to set the record straight, though I was only trying to protect his identity: his name's Billy, not Charley.

Other times, like the hound here called Dharma, the naming of animals can have unsettling effects. A ewe by here, from a blackface tup to a Hebridean ewe (I'm guessing) with black and white markings, has only an unofficial descriptive name. To burst into the bar then, to announce "the badger's had a lamb" can be the occasion for some puzzled looks among tourists.

Likewise, to encounter a man as it's getting dark, slamming his door behind him and setting off along the road yelling "Whisky!" is something summer visitors find only too believable of west-highland men. They don't stop long enough to learn that it's his dog's name.

6th

On the sea: a low guttural *r-rak* and moaning *moo-oo-airh*.

At the headland: croaking and retching, *frarnk* and a liquid bubbling trill *cour-li crwee croo-ee*.

In the oakwood: a cascade of notes ending with a flourish – *choo-ee-o* then *chwink wheet chwit* and a persistent scolding *wheet tsack tsack* and *tit tit tit* and a prolonged breathless jingle of high notes.

On the hill: a croaking clucking plainsong and a deep high metallic *prronk*.

In the sky: *pee-oo mee-oo.*

Birdsong is hard to approximate in our alphabet and there's a huge debate about its musical notation, with some commentators claiming that, Messiaen and Handel notwithstanding, it's nonsense to transcribe birdsong into Western 12-note scales, since they sing microtonally.

Charles Ives describes microtones as the notes between the cracks on a piano. For sure the "words" used to describe birdsong here, which I drew in part from Peterson, Mountfort and Hollom's *Birds of Britain and Europe*, my companion for all my adult life, are perhaps unrecognisable as the liquid languages of birds I encounter this morning on a walk to Port a' Bhata. It's also been argued that human music is a response to and (to begin with at least), an imitation of birdsong. There's no doubt that it's the same impulse that has me laughing and rasping aloud a fragment from the Song of the Volga Boatmen as I step yet again into ankle deep mud, slotted with deerprints along the path stags and hinds have trodden for how long.

Birdsong is a response, a pure clear communication of heart and mind and body together, spontaneous; and to hear, among hills and bays, is fathomless and silencing.

But nothing silences the possible.

10th

> *further in yet*
> *further in yet*
> *green hills*

> (Santoka, poet, hermit, sometime sake brewer, "good for nothing",
> Buddhist mendicant; translated by William J Higginson)

Today being Human Rights Day, I ponder more than usual the scream of the Tornado jet as it passes between Beinn Resipol and Beinn Bhàn west to east along Loch Sunart.

When I arrive at Camas a' Choirce, the sun has already dipped behind Beinn Bhàn, the big hill above Laudale on the other side of the loch in Morvern. Although only about 50 yards across the water here, Morvern is hours away on foot. I climb the slope to Resipole, through

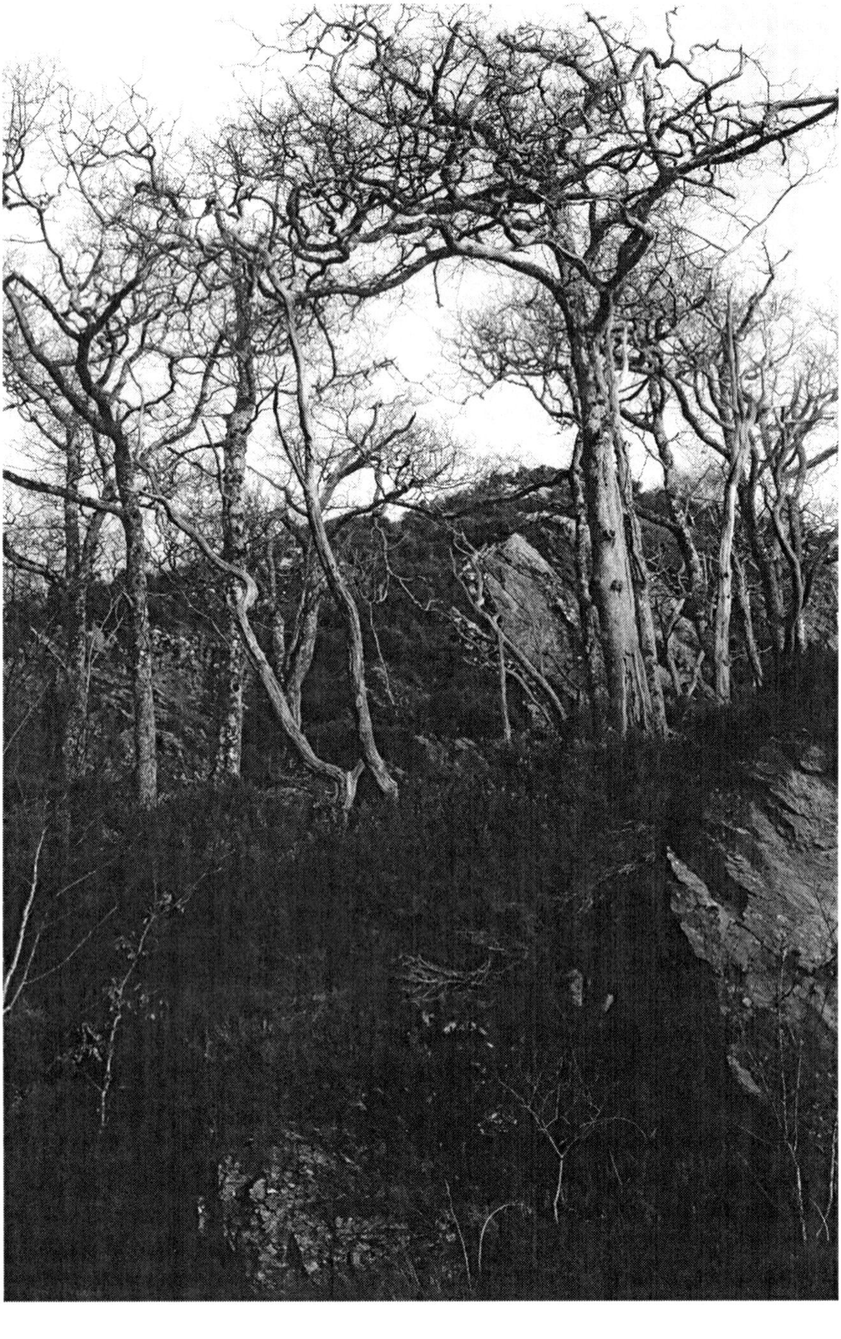

forestry and remnant oak forest where the gorges of Allt Camas a' Choirce (the bay of corn) and the rocks and gradients made it unprofitable for planting sitka spruce. Picking my way among the frost pockets which dissolve the bracken in winter's attrition, cracking the ice in standing water, crossing and crossing again the deep-cut burns to gain a little height, my pluming breath steams out, like any old horse at winter work, and beads spider webs. The burns, small but insistent, are feeders for the torrent in the gorge, here and there dropping off less worn rock edges in waterfalls. There's no sound here but the brawl of water – constant but rising and falling in cadence as I slowly make my way up alongside, now close enough to be splashed, now behind overhanging oaks, as the terrain dictates.

It was my intention to reach the snow line on Resipol, but when I finally clear the trees – my progress is slow, poking and peering, stopping and listening – I'm in the sun, having climbed higher than its angle behind Beinn Bhàn – and too hot in my sweater for the climb. The sweater, an Aran knit has just been darned for me by an expert in the village. It was made more than thirty years ago here in Argyll; it didn't wear out, but was attacked by moths. I mention it because round about the time it was made, I was panting up Carrauntoohill, Ireland's highest mountain, in my best tackety boots and met, near the top, after some particularly irritating scree, a man looking after his sheep. He had a cigarette in his mouth, and no more equipment than a flat cap and welly boots.

I sit on a rock outcrop that's bare among heather, smoothed and weathered over millennia, the kind that elsewhere in Argyll has been carved with enigmatic neolithic cup and ring marks. The flesh of the mountain. I sit for the best part of an hour, cooling, senses at a threshold level, simply receptive. When the sun starts blinking again behind the mass of the mountain, so do I. Resipol, at about 2,700 feet, is a Corbett, not so tall, but the snow seems to recede with each step I take and the rises between me and the peak seem to grow in number; I think of the poem by Santoka. I'm not concerned with mountain tops; faced with a choice of going further up, ice and snow above or down before dusk into frost, I take the path of the unhurried stag, preferring to leave the tops to their volcanic dreaming and move downhill, the body's song in my every step.

The oaks corkscrew on themselves, their lower branches brushing my head as I pass under. Undisturbed webs are thicker here; the trees wound with ivies, climbed by lungwort and lichens, buttressed with mosses, into which my singing springing steps sink. Among the oaks are scattered younger hollies and birches. Lower, the oaks are cracked, torn and broken by winds; they fall partly to lean on their fellows. Their slow growth still seeking the upright. Along the burn the deep quiet pools alternate with white spume as water hits bed boulders. The floor of the spruce plantation the other side is black and silent, only small creatures negotiating the tangle of branches down to knee height on a man. The boundaries we set are not held to: among the sitka are yearling hollies, their hard seeds perhaps passing through the gut of a songbird to grow where they land; among the oaks are sitka saplings, seed brought by wind and squirrel. Full of laughter I move faster downhill, tapping the bracket fungi on birches, a little dance past the last lime green leaves of low fraochan – the sweet blueberries of summer gone.

11th

A soft day. The southerlies seem to have brought milder weather, with harmless and haphazard smirrs of rain wetting nothing much. Matching that soft weather, I hear the calls of the ravens before I see them – a large silhouette flying across the hill just below my clear sightline attracts my attention and I'm momentarily puzzled when it swoops up as a buzzard. Then the two ravens appear and jink together, above and below the buzzard, sending it clear over the crest of Gobsheallach hill on an updraught of wind and curse. The raven pair then flies over to demonstrate possession of the entire south side of the hill. They might be performing a mating flight, such is their exuberance, wing to wing coasting, stopping short only of the upside down flight I associate with their mating. But I guess it's too early for that and they are just whooping it up a little after their effortless eviction of the buzzard.

It's their gentle glottal calls I enjoy the most – the triple *hyonk pyonk donk* followed by a musical note like striking a dry emptied small log with a heavy stick, a deep xylophonic note, a marimba and mallet. I'm entranced at their flight and their bonded ecolect, their overheard personal conversation.

By the bay, the thin peep and rising inflection of five oystercatchers, like so many whistling kettles, as they rise to settle twenty yards further along the tideline is uncertain quavering soprano to the tenor gargling of a solitary curlew.

13th

The south wind has reached a storm, though still without rain. Outgoing tide is crossed by the force of the wind, spray flying high.

Whiteness of lichen rings on oak and the stems of birches, their peeling bark white as my lover's thigh, stand against a sky black as spilled ink, a silhouette in reverse.

Clothes pegs clack luminously along the clothes line back and forth like the beads of an abacus. A crow, just blacker than the sky, is torn away from the hill by the updraught and swoops down to a hollow like any gathered leaf.

Lurid is very close to lucid.

16th

With the very short days now, sunrise at about nine o'clock and sunset at about half past three, giving six and a half hours of daylight, there is more of the night and consequently of the moon. The waxing half moon rises at noon and rides high in the sky most of this cloudless day until it slips behind the horizon thirteen hours later at one in the morning. Plates of surface ice hem the lochans all day.

    As well as the weather, of importance here is light and clarity. On this clear cold day, when every breath is felt deep into the lungs, there's much talk of how far can be seen and how clearly.

    As the sun rises, the hills make one black and broken line to the south; in full sunlight, they resolve into three clean lines of hills, one behind the other, receding in distinctness. Even now, towards dusk it's still clear. To the west, the hills of Rum make a jet profile against a low band of coral flushing the horizon. Overhead the high sky is a translucent duckegg blue. To the east and south the sun flares red on the hills, somewhere on the spectrum between the bracken and rusting plough at the grazing called Park and the flames of the fire burning the year's end scraps at the Kentra croft.

    As the sun sets, the lines of hills become one again against an ice-blue sky. Clarity dissolves to dark.

18th

It's light but the sun is not above the hills yet. Frost everywhere, from roof slates to the sheep-cropped grass, which is white, no shade of green. I set off across the brittle tussocks which only the highest tides cover. Tide last night was moderate and low was at half past five. I want to find out if the white out on the bay is ice. Coming off the salt flats I step onto frozen sand ridges which the sea has left. Wormcasts are frozen solid. Bladderwrack is frosted white. Any depressions in seabed (that's what I'm walking on – the point where land is reclaimed by the sea in its continual cycle) are filled with shallow sea ice. At twenty past nine the sun glows at the hill line. At this time of year it's so far south of east as to be disorienting; I think I've gone badly astray, a feeling heightened by the double blinding of the sun and its reflection in the iced sands. Squinting downward, I head directly into the sun, towards the three scattered islands where sometimes stranded sheep sleep in the summer, Eileanan Loisgte, the burnt islands. Another five minutes and the sun is clear of the hill and rising along its low arc. Even a couple of days from solstice where everything hangs and tilts, the brilliance is too much for me. I head into the black gloam of the islands and turn back along my footprints. My shadow, cast ahead, is thirty feet long. At this point, I'm in the middle of the bay among crackling mussel beds and the air's cracked, torn apart by a roar that goes to my nape; ahead of it goes the Tornado jet itself, which I only catch a glimpse of with its wing missiles. The noise is visceral. It bypasses everything rational and goes direct to the thalamus – seat of primal reaction. I crouch down, vulnerable on miles of open sand. There's no cover.

It passes. I straighten up and with the jet safely away shake my fist. I curse. Atavism recedes into the reptilian brain and I walk on back across acres of frost and ice, the weight of sky on the back of my neck. The mountains of Afghanistan are not so very far away. Not a bird stirs.

21st

The day before winter solstice and all the ice and frosts have melted. Down at the edge of the bay two donkeys softly graze at the regreened but salty grass. The sunlight is radiant and the unclouded sky a zinging blue. The donkeys are dark against all this. They're minded by a woman and a child. One is led from a grass cropping to the next; the other is free to roam, but stays close to his companion and the girl. Donkeys here in Ardnamurchan are a rarity these days, what ever might have been in the past. These are retired, though from what work I don't know.

It's more than thirty years since I backed a donkey into a donkey car to tackle him to bring in hay. While donkeys can be biddable, they always have minds of their own. Ours, a rig, had a habit of submitting to the collar, and backing up far enough to be tackled, then moving forward sharply so that the shafts dropped. The old TVO tractor that replaced him was not a lot better. It was commonplace at that time in Kerry for donkeys to take the milk from maybe a half dozen cows each day from the holdings to the collection point for the creamery lorry. Even then, they were being replaced by bulk tanks, coolers and tractors with cabs.

The donkeys here in Gobsheallach may never work and even on occasion bite, just to let you know their ancestry, but in the solstice sun here, now, there's plenty of grazing for them. In Palestine, since the checkpoints were rigorously (re)enforced there's not a lot of diesel or petrol getting into the West Bank or Gaza and donkeys are the general transport, serving as taxi and ambulance and draught animal. Beasts of burden. Grazing is scarce in a land one-fifth the size of Scotland but with more than two and a half million people. Many farms, frequently olive and citrus groves, have been annexed for a wall between Palestine and Israel; the trees are bulldozed and the land out of farming. On any other fertile ground, crops for people is the order of the day. Even with the price of a donkey twenty or thirty times what it was before the virtual sealing of the Palestinian lands, if grazing, or hay or concentrate can't be had, there's no future for donkeys in Ramallah or Hebron or Bethlehem.

24th

This one, the snow moon, wakes me at night; full and high. By day full double arcing rushing rainbows one above the other; in the spaces between grey showers and grey clouds, scraps of bows here and there on and off to the east and now to the west and then south. Waves of what is come together, coincide for a while and dissolve, in the sky as in the bay.

26th

Nine intoxicating things at Loch Sunart today

To stand in darkness rocked by a gale

Rain in the night

The order of birds that comes to finish morning hen food: three grey crows; a blown flock of chaffinches; one robin; four wood pigeons

The first lilac alder buds

Clubmosses

Foxglove rosettes

23 herons taking to the air and wheeling for 3 awe-long minutes, huge against sky above Garbh Eilean before landing to sit in rain like random boulders on a rock outcrop, muttering in convocation.

The raised head of a single seal at the same place from the sea

Water blueing after grey with the traverse of rain along the loch

28th

At night I sleep dreaming under goose down. Heavy in the early morning on the peat bog I'm mazed by a solitary goose struggling to get airborne – a mastery of muscle and pneumatic bone over gravity – and when she's joined by a vibrant honking hooting cavalcade of score upon score, following in an untidy raggle of flight, up, yapping up – then for me, awake now, it's also willing them aloft to circle and make off celebrating life and flight; uplifting and uproarious all at once.
    There's two sorts of goose here, the barnacle, all black and white and the grey lag, with its pink bill. This enormous gaggle is the largest I've seen; up to a hundred birds. I'm still smiling as the skeins make off to the south barking all the way; and at four to five pounds weight each bird

I'm still lost at the power of feather-clad muscle; each of my watery steps across the bog makes sucking noises accentuating my weight, my pressure on the goose feeding grounds.

29th

There is a need to approach Sunart oakwoods obliquely. Like sitting. Sitting very still, alert and relaxed, waiting for something to arrive: a deer, maybe, or an owl. If I look at trees in the dusk directly, they dance in vision; it's the way our eyes are physically made. Look to one side and the tree is clearer. I approach trees sideways, a little nervous of their history and presence. I count geese, deer, list mosses, enumerate spiders, look out to sea with my back to the woods, holly and birch and alder all around. It's as if to look directly is to somehow obscure a latency, a voice that I want to listen to; but it's not enough to be attentive, scientific; it's necessary to be receptive. I'm impatient. I'll not live as long as an oak.

30th

In Cill Chaluim Chille,
near the Camerons and MacLeods,
among the MacLeans and MacInneses,
in 'the big graveyard above Loch Alainn',
I chanced on MacLachlan's grave,
not knowing it was there.

I know fine well where John MacLachlan, the Doctor of Rahoy is buried, since Sorley MacLean writes of it in his praise poem. I also know that there's another grave over at Rahoy, and that intrigues me, as there's no church or burial ground there.

The day's not good for a foray to Rahoy, the other side of Loch Sunart at the inside length of Loch Teacuis; wet, cold, grey and blustery, but the grave is calling and I want to see what the Doctor would recognise there 130 years after his death.

At Kinlochteacuis birches and oaks show a distinct tendency for corkscrewing their growth into the air with the passing years, which I've noticed elsewhere in the woodlands, but it's a clear pattern here.

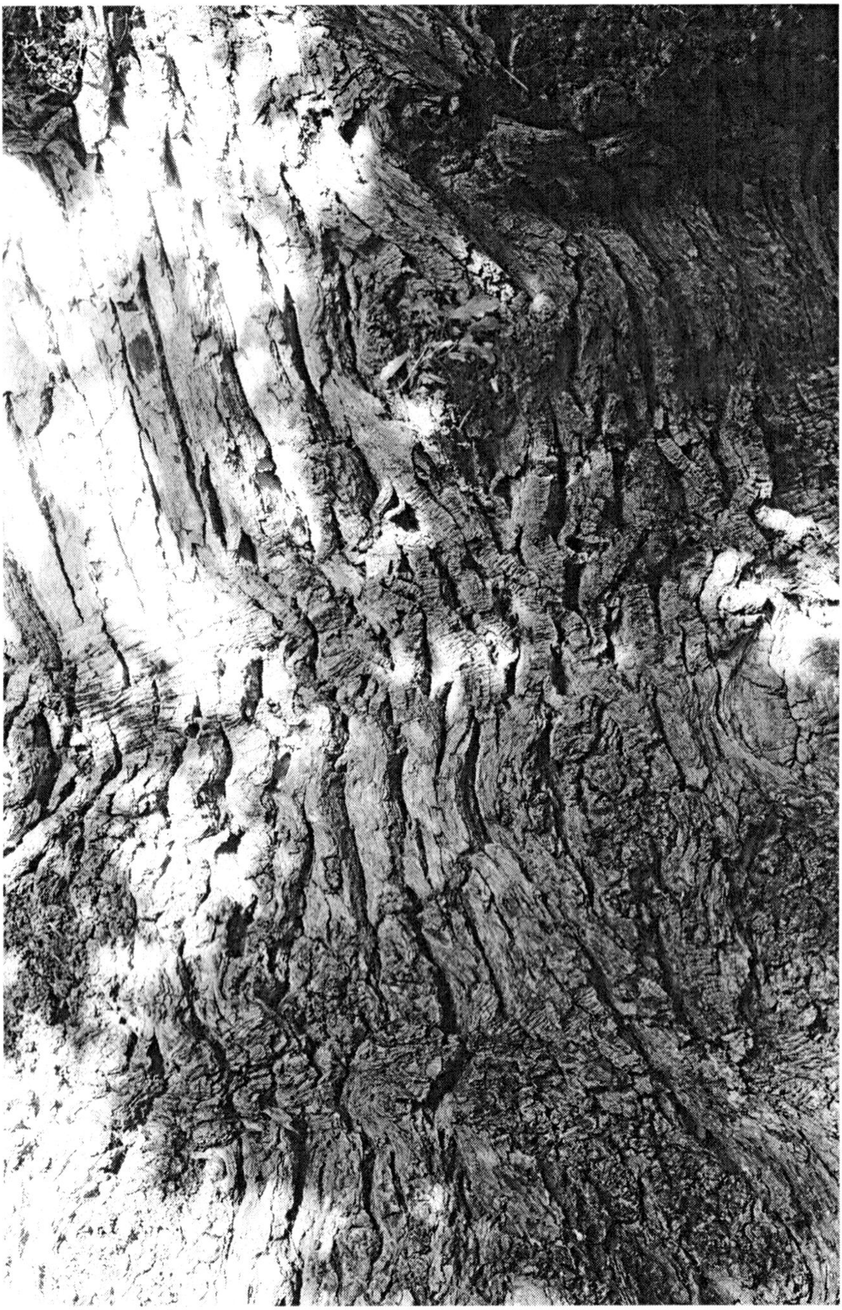

Despite the wet and the cold and the season, the woodbine is beginning to tenderly leaf and, oddly, there's some delicate white bramble blossoms. Spring may come early for its own reasons, but the first signifiers I see have the imprimatur of ownership – Estate signs with *stay away* as a not quite hidden undernote: Private Road, Deerstalking in Progress During …the usual dreary preoccupation of people taken with the notion that Rahoy (and Kinlochteacuis, Morvern, Ardnamurchan, Scotland outside cities) is a sporting estate for the enjoyment of a few whose traditions enable them to escape thought and conscience.

> *"…I cannot get a plot in my native country*
> *though I'd pay a crown for a mere shoe-breadth."* writes the Doctor.

As the rains wet the woods and hills indiscriminately, my thoughts, gloomy to begin, are lifted by the knowledge of the reefs in Loch Teacuis here, which John MacLachlan probably never saw, but neither do the current landowners have control of. The land and sky is grey, but there are rare serpulids beneath the grey loch water, at only ten feet down.

The home of tubeworms, the shell-like reefs twist up from the seabed at perhaps the same rate of growth as the corkscrewing birch and oak on the slopes that move down below sea level. There's only four sites in the world for *Serpula vermicularis* reefs. The worm's colours, bright red and orange, displayed in bronchial crowns outside the coral-like tubes, brighten my day immeasurably. Even the MacLachlan one would have smiled, taking a moment from his sadness and anger at landowners' disregard of his culture.

The squalls set in once again from the southwest, with dusk not far behind. The grave, when I find it near the dun, is to a Naval officer who died in 1933, fifty nine years after John MacLachlan, and who is buried under a stone cairn topped with a cross. Nearby ("not knowing it was there") I find another, newer grave, of a young Army Captain who died while climbing Ben Nevis in 2000, Colin Campbell his name.

The irony of a Captain Campbell's final resting place being Morvern would not be lost on the Doctor; who knew very well of the burnings on the Morvern coast: a retribution against those who joined the Jacobite cause in 1745. Philip Gaskell in Morvern Transformed records: "On the 10th instant, (March 1746) at four in the morning" [the writer is Captain Duff, in charge of the sloops Terror and Princess Anne, after having burned every boat he could find on the coast of Morvern and

Loch Sunart, in a letter to the Duke of Argyll] " I landed Lieut. Lindsay … [and] Captain Campbell with twinty men from Mingary Castle, a lieutenant and fifty five men from my ship with orders to burn the houses and destroy the effects of all such as were out in the rebellion." [Camerons, MacLeans, MacLeods] "They began with Drumnin M'Clean's town and by six o'clock at night they had destroy'd the Morvern coast as far as Ardtornish." As well as 400 houses, several barns "well fill'd with corn, horse, cows and meal" [adds Captain Hay, another RN officer] were torched. The woodlands surrounding that entire part of the coast also went in flames – a scorched earth policy for sure – and in the ensuing two centuries, whatever else has been healed, the woodlands from Drimnin to Lochaline have never fully recovered.

The Doctor would not know the houses, holiday cottages, here today (and I suspect he may have been as bemused as me by the welded steel stag on the big house lawn) but he would recognise the heavy hand of alleged landownership. The hills, the loch, the woods, remain unchanged.

In the scant oakwoods of Rahoy, Captain Campbell's grave is marked by the planting of half a dozen small specimens of what looks to be an exotic species of pine, clustered round the bronze plaque and seat with fine views along Loch Teacuis and the hills.

My way home is lit by the white throat of a pine marten crossing the path.

2008

January
1st

When the tide's at its lowest, it's possible to walk straight out on the sea bed, north along the Black Sea-Ford for half a mile towards the island and small skerries in the South Channel. With no mark of a footprint on the sand except for the tracings the various sea vegetables make as they are swung back and round by the ebb tide. These vary from circles to what looks like a small child's drawing of a three eyed elliptical alien, but is only an impression of bladderwrack drawn by the sea. Otherwise, no curlew has passed this way, no oystercatcher. Sometimes a stag or hind will pass here, but it's a little soft today and they're elsewhere in the hills grazing, sleeping, at this hour before dusk. It's just ten days since solstice and already there's a little more light in the mornings and even more noticeably in the evening, when the day is extended by about half an hour.

I head for the promontory of the MacNeill, across from the promontory of the Dividing, though of what I've no notion, unless it's one set of broken skerries and mud sand flats, one set of salt flats and shoals and yet others to the west; though perhaps also defines the bounds of land-use and tenancy. It's along from Port Ban and I want to walk as far out into the sea as it's possible to get without a dinghy. The promontory when I reach it is sodden with the rains. Not just the past week or month, but of the centuries. Itself a rock into the channel, from whose bed it rises up, cracked and worn by sand-laden wind, in its twisting and walking and weatherings it has developed hollows in which water lies, covered by sphagnums rotting into what, given greater depth and another thousand years could become peat.

Skirting the deepest moss hags, given away by the red moss growing patchily among the green and yellow rising sphagnum, sticking to the bare rock and the few patches of soft rush which give a firm foothold, I crest the slight rise to look out to the open sea, beyond the shoreline of tumbled rocks and rounded tide-blackened boulders. There, at this point where no one goes from one year's end to the next, a silhouette against the glare of the ocean surface, is a man knee-deep in waders, I guess fishing.

As I stand wondering whether to abandon the walk and make for the eastern headland after all, he slowly swivels his head and reveals the massive curve of an eagle's beak. The sun had fooled me, along with the glare and conditioning of my kind to see human figures in the landscape. But there's no doubt about it and a hesitant step or two carefully avoiding any more of the skyline shows me this cracked and unvisited landscape is hers, not mine.

Her three-foot height is also bulky enough to have fooled me, but stood on top of a low boulder facing the sea she appears much taller. A heron swings away to the north and to the east a noisy pack of oystercatchers chatters by, piping their grumbles to the world. She's still as I am, unmoved, focussed, her profile still to the west. I hold my breath, move closer, but even above the noise of the cold wind she has heard my squelchings and scrabbling on rock, and her head swivels a little further and I'm caught in that crisp and cogent stare. Without a word, I'm as apologetic as I would be having disturbed any new year angler; but she doesn't trust me and I'm far too close at less than thirty feet, and she rises slightly, spreads her wings, which are so huge, I feel they would umbrella the distance between us, and takes off in a single flap and a long glide towards the big island north. She reveals a white tail and I take a breath as I realise what I should have known all along from her size – she's a sea eagle. She dwarfs the skinny heron still making across the channel and is over, I think before I draw breath again, to disappear among rocks her own colour.

I sit, exhilarated; take a swig of malt from the flask in wonder and elation, and the seals edge together slightly. Throughout the drama, for it can best be called that: the facing of eagle and man, the seals have been as unnoticed as any other rocks, not fidgeting as they often do, silent, dozing. But the tension's ended, and something has changed for them in the charged air and they yawn themselves awake and then back to sleep.

Frances Pitt, writing in 1946 had seen the last nesting place of the sea eagle in Britain, the west cliffs of North Roe in Shetland. A pair nested there every year until 1908, when a local farmer shot the male. The female, a partial albino, returned each spring until 1918, after which she was seen no more. In 1947, Frank Fraser Darling writes of the sea eagle and its disappearance from Mull, Jura, Eigg, Skye, and the Shiants: "It is all a dismal story; and it is a matter for doubt whether, should these species try again to colonize this country, they would be allowed to breed in security. The vested interests of game preservation (by no means dead in a Socialist Britain), of a decrepit sheep-farming industry, in the West Highlands and Islands, the pressure of egg collectors and irresponsible gunners, are heavy odds."

Not only are the vested interests of game preservation still strong, but they have seen off the attempt at a "socialist Britain". Sheep farmers have changed however. My neighbours here, the man and woman of the croft were as pleased to see a sea eagle as I would have been, and it standing by the phone box at the road junction where no houses are for a quarter mile in any direction. Maybe it was expecting a call from Rum, which lies seven miles offshore, and where sea eagles were reintroduced in 1975, breeding from 1985. They've grown in numbers, though they are slow breeders, and spread a little in the past twenty three years, but there's still only about two hundred individuals across the Small Isles, Mull and hereabouts.

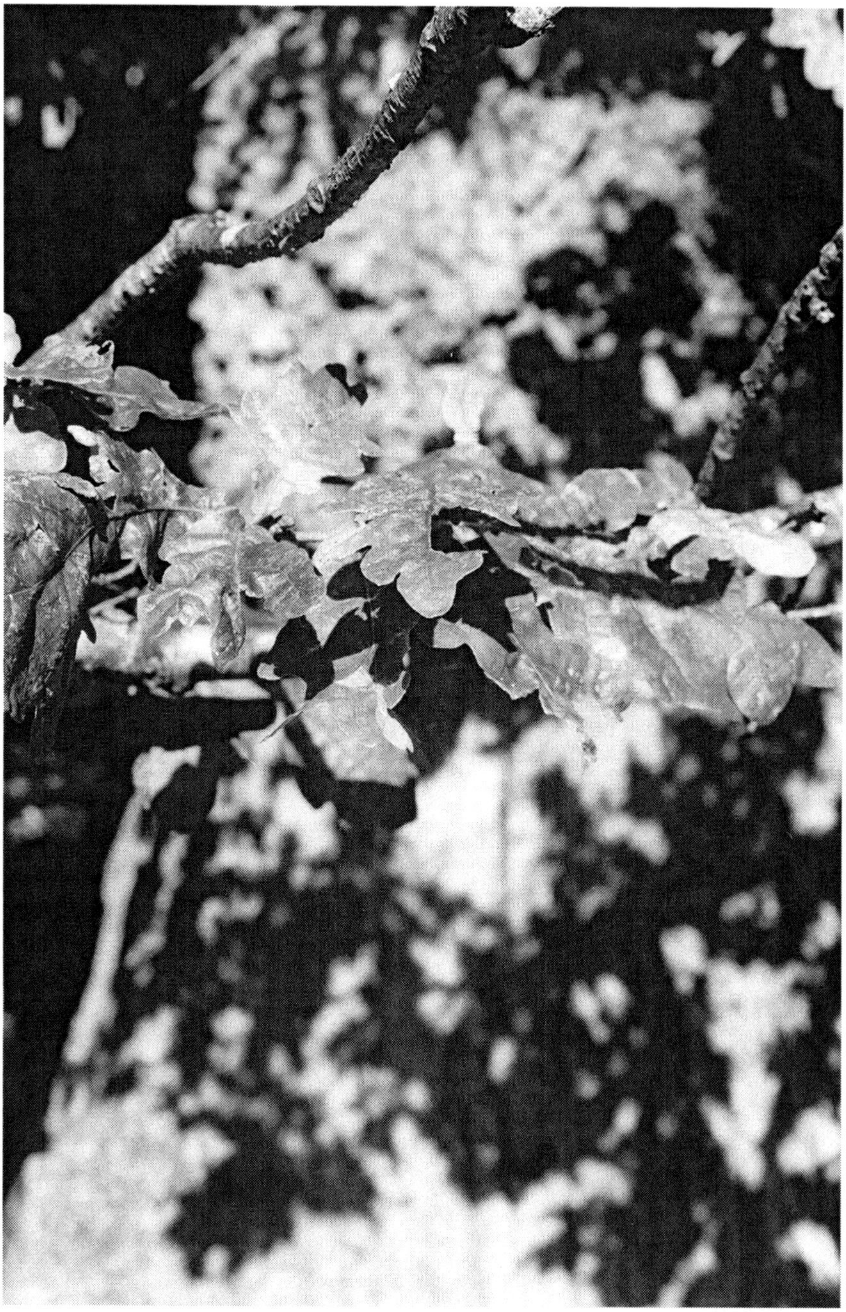

8th

> *Even when you take to the woods,*
> *you're taking political steps*
> *on political grounds.*
> *Apolitical poems are also political,*
> *and above us shines a moon*
> *no longer purely lunar.*
>   Wisława Szymborska

Away in the city for a day, captured by its busyness, bludgeoned by noise, I return through the blizzards home. Beinn Resipol, white in the night sky, lights my way as surely as a crescent moon.

It's not an escape here, but an engagement with the world as it is; something that's not entirely as we have determined it to be. It's just more apparent in Ardnamurchan that we have built over the rotting layers of sandstone and pitchstone, over the black basalt. Geology is obvious here, the topography where we settle in the hollows away from a climate predominantly of wind and rain. The woodlands have naturally been exploited and manipulated, the beasts and plants who live in, on, and around them exploited too.

This world, though, as it presents itself more clearly than elsewhere in a wholly built environment. It's as well to engage and re-engage with small sounds that punctuate the quiet: the greenfinch darting for crumbs outside the byre, the hirpling grey crow making a single note before rising idly away as I walk by, reed buntings *tseek-tseeking* their calls back and forth, sleet falling onto the bare branches and boles of the oaks. Domestic noises too: after the power cut the click of the hotplate and the creak and groan of the heating kettle.

And the things whose noises I don't hear, simply take in with silent eyes – the white capping of each hill from here to Morvern, and north to Moidart, the glisten of the tidal flats in the bay, below which live the worms whose songs are of dark and of crackling salt.

I'm at the top of the chain that starts below the worms and their subterranean songs, a chain (rather a web) of mutual dependence, of symbiosis and clear ecological interdependence. That knowledge is a barn full of riches. It's also the wealth on which cities are built, and it's here that I fully engage with that.

As a child, I pictured the ancient Greeks as philosophers walking back and forth, or standing still, lost in thought, dressed in loose robes, scattered across rolling hills bathed in sunlight. To enter the sloping woodlands this morning is to enter that place of my early imagining; the oaks sombre and silent, the random holly trees fresh with their green, aspens whitely standing and all apace on the hill, occupying precisely the positions of the philosophers, with here and there a rowan and an alder twined in earnest debate. Some have stood still so long that their feet have become buried in moss, which creeps up their boles to knee height; their limbs speckled with lichens like the liver spotted skins of the very old. Like any dialectic, winter has revealed the woodland armature, demonstrating, *enacting*, structure and formation of organic growth.

Here I have found the world as it is and also as it was for that child; a place of myth and of undisputed poetry, a place that has its location wherever I am properly awake and fully engrossed, enmeshed in things – which may be another definition of *politic*.

9th

The dog in the newspaper is said to flow from the trap at 40mph. The picture alongside the story shows a handsome brown dog wearing two collars. I'm not sure why two collars, but then any dog that fast can presumably wear as many collars as he likes. Like the hound here and myself, he appears to be quite indolent when he's not winning races. He rises early, but simply to breakfast on toast and soup. His only exercise is a two mile walk and a 300 metre gallop on the straight. The hound on the sofa at ten years old does more than that and so do I, though I do without the gallop. I'd love to know how fast the gently snoring couch-hound can move. She certainly has almost caught a hind now and then. Maybe I'll organise a time trial on the sands one day; it might be difficult, since she only runs in a circle with me at the middle.

I'd left the hound behind to go out for air between squalls (she hates weather), but the crofter, her dog, the one with the same name as the postman's baby (the old one that is. Postman, not baby. We have a new postman now. I don't think there's any connection.) : that dog loups up behind me and insists on tagging along a way, flushing snipe and looking round at me, tongue hanging, white tail-plume aloft, as though we're partners. In these cold January days, with snow on the hills, I'd like to think he can also feel the spring just ahead of us or behind the old oak trunk, somewhere there. But I guess he simply needs to stretch his legs like me, and I'm his alibi for wandering away from the croft. We stand and look out at the bay, curlews and all, with not a word passing between us, a companionable silence as dusk gathers itself, with a squall moving in across the Atlantic. We turn at the same time to get back before the sleet, but it overtakes us anyway as we knew it would. At the byre, the slates of the house over by are turned gold in the sulphurous and nicotine light of the whirling weather front and the hillside bracken a scarlet as deep as any autumn rowan berry.

So the short days pass and the dog and I part company at the door – me for a dram, him for chasing a pickup moving along the hill to the croft house

12th

The Sgurr Biorach is the highest sgurr,
but Sgurr nan Gillean the best sgurr,
the blue-black gape-mouthed strong sgurr,
the tree-like slender horned sgurr
the forbidding great dangerous sgurr,
the sgurr of Skye above the rest.
           Sorley MacLean

The rain and squalls stopped yesterday and the sky turned blue. Frost rose from the ground very hard, under a sky in which every star could be plucked and the Milky Way spilled itself north. This morning is clear and cold and the road to Ardtoe is icy. The sun is about as high as it ever gets at this time of year and shining on the sea leads over to Eigg and beyond Eigg, to the little peaks of Rum. They are all wearing snow on their heads and haunches and from this distance, maybe twenty miles, are of a perfect and delicate volcanic symmetry. They are set in a clear sapphire ocean and lead me further, over the hatchery dams, across the tide-low sands of Sailean Dubh, over the inland machairs: inland only so far as they are sheltered by west facing rocks. Where the tide has retreated, it has left goblet-thin sheets of ice across tussocks and over departed pools. Compelled forward by a need to see more of the islands, since I'm now at sea level, but with no sight beyond the nearest rocks, I move crabwise round Carn Mor, where the black terrier bitch that belongs here, to the man of the fishing boat, joins me. Like me, she picks her way delicately: frosted moss has a very thin crust. Where she senses a depth of water, she detours the long and drier way round. I move up and down, still skirting the Carn, past all the headlands – Rubha Fassadh nam Feocullan (which I take to mean the place of the pine marten), Rubha na Clioche Bàine, Rubha na Caillich round nearly to Rubha Mhic Artair. and there, when I finally get a clear view west are the islands: flat little Muck the southernmost, Eigg of course, with its own sgurr and guarding it from the worst Atlantic gales, the hills of Rum. But to the north are the Cuillins and Skye laid out as a summer's day, north and slewing round out of sight to the west behind the great sgurrs of Sorley Maclean's poem; Sgurr Biorach and Sgurr nan Gillean, Sgurr na Stri, Sgurr nan Eag and Sgurr Alastair with Sgurr a' Ghreadaidh; their names a litany of solitude and geology; places known best by those who live there – eagles, buzzards, ravens and crows – but which pierced MacLean's heart.

The way round the Carn is to move from the islands' stilling presence, eastwards and inland along the south channel, Eilean Shona to the north. I've hunted the small terrier away: I have no knowledge of how she is with sheep, and I'm heading for Fhaodhail Dhubh where the sheep wander at will. I cross the burn at Port na Lathaich with its little groves of snapped and dead birches, the sky punctured by the ravens' silhouettes and the rush of the water an arrhythmic counterpoint to the soft and melodious *prunk prunk* of the ravens discussing such a one as myself edging across the hill of the brush.

13th

The sea, at the little boathouse along by the jetty near Ardtoe, has offered me a plank. It is five feet long and ten inches wide, with, at each end, the remains of three evenly spaced screws, loosened in their holes by the hammering of onshore surf. It's as well not to refuse what the ocean offers, because it as easily takes away. This plank I welcome. It has clearly been in the sea a long time, heavy with salt, washed about the coast before the currents and recent gale stranded it here. It's broken along one edge, which I can easily saw to make straight and true again as the tree once reached up. It's pine. I'm guessing it did not grow in Sunart, though its history is uncertain. Once, is all I know, it was part of a tree; now planked and dressed it has a swaggering air, like any sailor at port. I'll dry it, use it on my live-aboard boat, as a part of the small dresser which needs to be built to take the Japanese biscuit barrel, the teacups and saucers, remaining china from my mother's long-ago wedding. It will be sanded, oiled to show its sweep of grain, with its story of summers and winters past for those who read such things; living again and at home again as part of a boat, since that's surely where it made its first home as plank. Next to the future dresser is the stove. Aldo Leopold writes that there are two dangers in not owning a farm. The second is of supposing that heat comes from a furnace. The offcuts from this plank will help fire up the stove for the baking of bread or the boiling of the kettle, to bring into play those teacups which will sit on the dresser's dressed plank. The heat of the pine trimmings will momentarily warm me, the teakettle, the water in the boiler and the boat herself.

I'll be sitting, mind working all this in woodland, wondering if the sawn tree itself is from the Baltic or maybe – and here imagination makes a little leap – from the Scots pine I could not find at Bun Allt Eachain that Alastair Cameron writes of in his *Annals*. Either way, I'll glean more than the plank; I'll guess where the tree grew that works so hard to give a glow in several dimensions.

17th

> it starts of course
> with the *finished* product.
> *nothing* starts with the 1st.
> Nothing. The end
> is first. Always.
> There is no beginning
> unless the end
> has been reached. First.
>
> Ed Dorn (A Theory of Truth / *The North Atlantic Turbine*

Sunart oakwoods are what they are because (among other factors like high rainfall) of the southern ocean's heat borne here from the Gulf Stream, along the North Atlantic Drift, travelling thousands of miles, cooling a little on the way, to invigorate our coastlines. These gloomy days, the Drift is perhaps threatened by icemelt entering the Atlantic and moved south by Greenland Sea currents. A cooling of the North Atlantic Drift could have strange and unguessed effects on the oakwoods, with temperatures perhaps falling by 5 degrees; though there may be increased rainfall, which might or might not counteract the drop in temperature.

The ecosystems we share with ocean current and climate are as fragile as wrens' eggs. Last spring at Ardtoe the crofter was piking loads of the sea's weeds from the foreshore into his trailer for the potato crop on his sandy soil, as Highlanders have done for generations; six hundred cartloads for a small croft each spring not being unusual. The weed in question was a *Laminaria (digitata)* which I've taken myself in smaller quantities for drying and adding to stock for soup. It's every bit as good as the Japanese variety *Laminaria saccharina* which can be bought now at great cost in delis and "health food" shops. This *saccharina* is found here too, but is less common. There's another *Laminaria – bulbosa*, that I've not found, appearing as it does only at equinoctial low tides and which Fraser Darling describes as "rather like coarse tripe turned inside out". The *Laminarias* are also the chosen delicacy of sea urchins, whose skeletons, or fragments of, are washed up on all the open Atlantic shores here, common wherever the Atlantic Drift licks the shallows. These graceful creatures have an exoskeleton no larger than the size of a small apple, covered in spines and deep purple or pink. The mouths of urchins are underneath the skeleton and have five beak-like teeth for nothing much other than scraping seaweed.

If the North Atlantic Drift were to cool further, or divert slightly because of wind, what would become of these creatures, who depend on its warmth; what would happen to their food-source and my stock?

Build a better mouse trap, they say. At Ardtoe, what I took to be a fish hatchery (it's that too) turns out to be breeding sea urchins. They have twenty or thirty of both *Paracentrotus lividus*, the purple sea urchin and *Echinus esculentus*, the "edible" sea urchin. Edible here refers to us humans eating urchins, not in any Swiftian sense, but the sea creatures; though in Brittany, the urchin of choice is the *Paracentrotus*, (oursin violet) which is lightly boiled in plenty of salt water for two minutes, then cracked and eaten like a boiled egg. The purpose at Ardtoe, though is not culinary, but for urchins' scavenging qualities.

The plan, with the aid of the millions of eggs these urchins produce, is to stock waters around farmed salmon cages, where they will eat particles of fish food which have escaped the salmon in such large quantities, that together with their excreta, make the seas murky for divers. The urchins will also be fed seaweed, *Laminaria* and *Alaria* (probably *esculenta*, used until recently here and in Ireland in soups – I know this as oarweed) which will be bred specifically for this purpose.

All this mouse trapping activity is of course about financial feasibility. We like to eat salmon, but there's too many of us, and salmon increasingly move towards extinction; no longer swimming inshore "thick enough to walk on" like a huge flock of underwater passenger pigeons. We invent then the farming of salmon, but the salmon cages pollute the seas. We breed urchins to clean the ocean around fish farms. To help the urchins on, sea vegetables are bred. This could be "viable on a commercial scale": urchins and weeds sold to fish farms, salmon sold to supermarket.

I'm not sure where this cycle leads; if urchins, *Laminaria* and *Alaria* can be eaten by us, (and in harder times were) where might that leave the salmon and their farmers if we all took to eating them. How would Tesco market small purple spiny creatures and sea vegetables that would be pungent in a very short time from harvest? How long before we need to clean up after urchins? What will happen to fish, urchin, sea weeds and oak woods if the North Atlantic Drift cools and our climate with it?

The story of the tree surviving because it is too crooked, gnarled and cracked to be of any use to the carpenter also possibly applies to sea creatures. It seems they'll only survive our predations if they are inedible to us.

FISH PRICES

Hake 60p-£7.50; plaice 60p-£2.50; cod £2-£3.40; lemon sole £1; whiting 20p-£1.40; sole £7.40-£14; roker 60p-£2.20; John Dory 50p; coley £1.20-£1.40; red mullet 60p-£4 (kg); megrim £3.50-£6; ling £1.50-£1.80 (kg).

As ever, monks (£2-£3.50) and witches (£3) everywhere.

Boats: Provider, Gratitude, Bountiful, Just Reward, Ocean Bounty. Also landing fish: Avocet and Osprey III.

19th

What do we call the shimmer of sea, each platt and wavelet, as tide pours in? What word do we have for the shadow of a white birch limb on cracked white-lichened rock?
The wolf moon is bulbous, slung low over Moidart's crumpled hills. Two curlews raise their pibroch plaint of wild poetry and are gone.

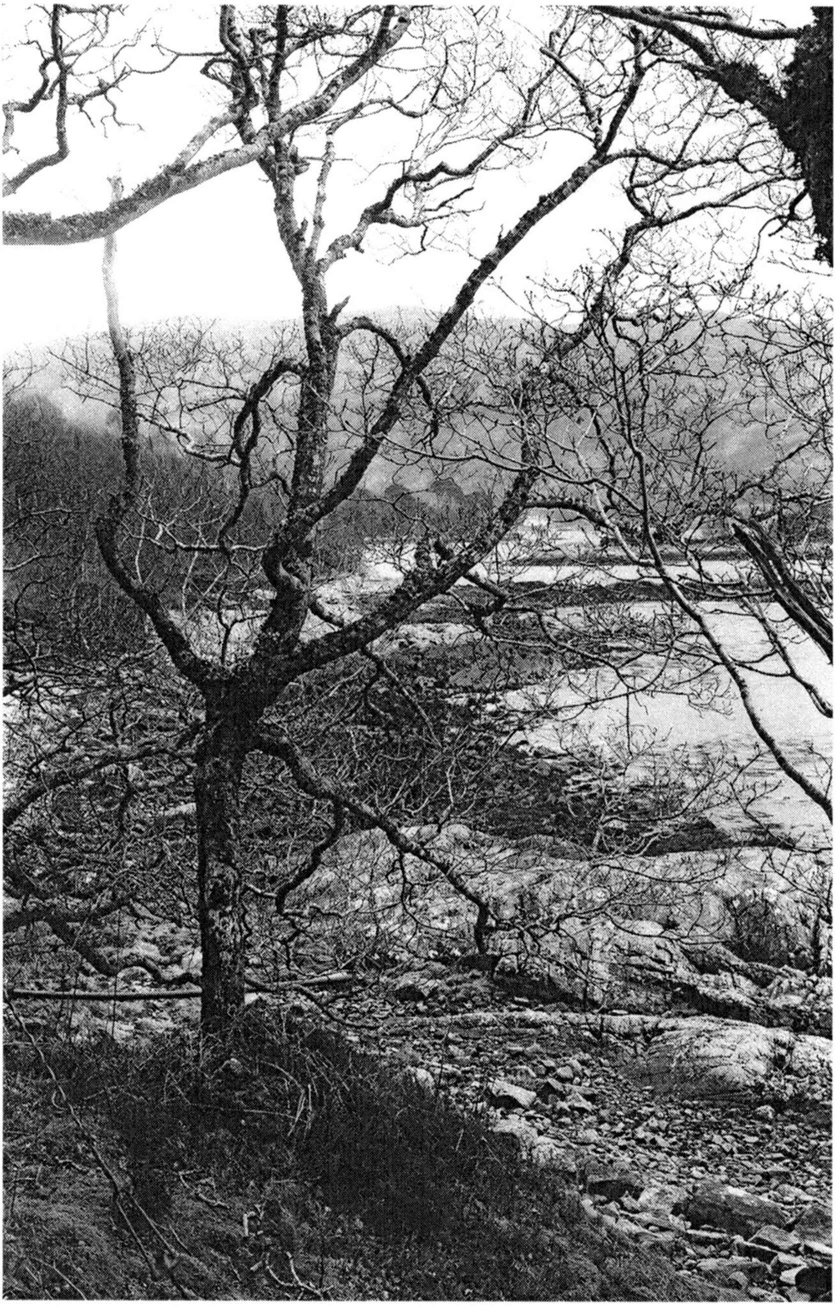

23rd

The three hinds were passing outside the window again, moving easily and alert from east to west. They're the same three I've been seeing at this hour of the early morning for a week or more. I've no real idea of the range of deer. I know they are hefted to a particular territory, but the size of the hill-ground, and in their case the bog, they consider theirs to occupy I can only guess at. I've seen them two miles from here to the east at dusk. They are easy to recognise, always three and one considerably smaller than the other two.

So this morning, giving a good half hour's start so as not to alarm them in any way, I follow the three sisters (as I think of them). They'd outrun me and I mean them no harm, but I want to try to track them in their usual day's routine. They need to cross the little road across the hill here, so I'm looking for their run, mindful that there are no sheep on the hill just now, so runs would be likely made by these three.

And there, where there's the most shelter between the birches, leading from just beyond a stand of alders, is their line. I follow the meander of a path. They seem not to mind the boggy patches in hollows, which suck at my feet more than their small cloven hooves, though they must sink further, the way a high heeled woman would. But it makes the slots easier to follow, and the dark droppings here and there, show a regular route. I come across beaten down patches of bracken in dips, where they must overnight sometimes. Sometimes a bite has been taken from a low fraughan, blaeberry. The track's leading up in a spiralling kind of way, west and up. The going is colder and rockier and of course I lose the track. Not before, however, working out that their only route needs to be to head back eastward round the curve of hill; that or walk off into the ocean.

Deer do seem to enjoy mooching on the sands here and there. I've seen them often enough, not browsing the sea's weeds like the sheep, but rather contemplating waves. But here there's no sand, just drops from the rocks. I've travelled only maybe a mile and a half and not very high, but the direction suggests that they will head back to where I see them at dusk, keeping the sea to their left, circumambulating the hill to make for the lower bog and the degree or so extra warmth and the shelter it brings. They'll be slowing down a little, with the calf each carries, half way through the gestation period, maybe not too picky about food, a little hungry; but nevertheless their occupancy of this limited stretch of hill and bog, bounded by the Atlantic, would seem to make a walk-round of about eight miles, taking in some three thousand acres of homeland, if my calculations are correct.

With the coverage of trees and rocks, with their ability to see and catch scent of me, their autumn bracken colouring and wariness, it's no surprise that I see their traces more often than their presence.

23rd / 24th *slipstream*

There's a hunger that compels at this lean time of year. The hinds feel it in scarcity, driven to feed the calves they carry, growing. The bared woodlands, framework for light made leaf, through terminal buds' grope away from last summer towards another spring. I feel an urgency to make marks to represent all this. To re present before present is past. To signify the fleeting thin things of winter.

I'd wanted to make maps. A map marking seasons' boundaries. A map that counteracted the victories of mapmakers, perhaps. A map that marked cleared villages here: Smirisary, Port a Bhata, Buarblaig, Inniemore, Uladail, burial grounds mossed over. A map of stories told by placenames, when story and tradition translated is no more than a loss.

I'd make a map of the boroughs and colonies of woodants – a story of community going and coming. A map of badger setts. Another of where the woodbine scrambles in its tangled way through branches of oaks; a map of the homes of the insects that make different kinds of oak-gall their home. Another of April's early purple orchids. An underwater map that left aside the numbers on a chart, which show only depth in metres; the lives of tubeworms and mussels have depth for those who feel that imperative hunger.

But of course the oak or the birch is a map of itself. Lichens stain the trunks, mosses clamber the boles, worts and ferns and microfauna consider it a territory, an occupancy, a home and commonwealth.

The circumambulation of the hinds round Carn Mor may be the start of our art. Quartered, crossed, marked with hoofprints. We map ourselves in a physical act, not reverential but existential. The first art of the circle, of cup and ring marks on stone; the art of palaeolithic hand prints in ochres from earth.

My hind tracking is a wonder at the art of creatures in a territory – inhabitants of a map which is not distinct from their selves. The present can't be re presented. Experience and memory impel the hinds in their search for sustenance and constrain me to my appreciation of their mapped world, from which I derive a feeding for the breathy spirit.

24th

The drama of the night is the moon, a night after full, navigating high, with gale tattered clouds mottling its surface. Several times gusts waken me and the moon is still there, as large an appearance in the night as truth retained from dream. The booming in the house has fooled me a few times, too, thinking that someone is banging the door to get in. At one point I'm at the front to make sure that the gate is shut and it isn't the flock looking for shelter.

The morning dawns on blizzards, with a full and high tide; white is everywhere. The sun makes brief guest appearances, but with the force of the wind, the clouds are driven in again, blackening the very brief clear spells. By mid morning, growling thunder has stepped up its volume and is now exploding round the hills. When the sky's at its darkest, hail rattles the small branches and topmost twigs, battering on down, stinging noses and muzzles alike.

The day moves on, with curtains rising and falling on weather scenes. The woods, usually noisy with bird calls, a twittering of chaffinches, is silent. The bay and sea and skerries, normally full of clamouring oystercatchers and burbling curlews, is silent. Bare bones of trees make grinding noises against each other in high wind. Only a pair of buffeted siskins moves, low down, fossicking for seeds, flighting close to the ground as I approach.

Hazel catkins seem to fold on themselves in the cold. Only the rhododendrons, those natives of Spain and Lebanon, with their spurts of growth since I last passed here and with their new terminal buds, seem aware of a spring that might arrive one day soon.

28th

It's as well to have a pocket full of seeds. Last month I travelled to visit family and this afternoon pulled on the old Donegal jacket I wore then, to make the happy rediscovery of maple seeds I had stashed. I'd been amusing the family toddlers by throwing the seeds in the air to watch them whirligig down with little rises in the puffing wind. None of us could get enough, marvelling at these patterns and the dissemination of purest opulence.

Last autumn wherever I went in the woodlands I collected seeds. Oak and hazel mostly, which have spent all winter in my fridge. Now, with the time come to stratify them (some would have done this immediately, but I'm in no hurry, nor are the seeds), I've been casting around for a container that neither the hens nor sheep will upturn or rootle about in.

The sheep are fresh on the hill, released from the gated Park, foraging like me, nuzzling the salty sand piles the road men leave for icy weather. Mooching around with no set purpose, still foraging for seeds even now, there by the boathouse is a plastic blue shallow fish tray. It's washed up on last night's tide and perfect for sand and seeds, with uniform holes to let the water through. It's under my oxter before I really think about it. I saunter home, an Ardnamurchan flâneur, with sea riches, thinking of the wealth of germination and the first leaves to come and dreaming of a tree nursery for these parts.

February
2nd

It's been snowing hard since yesterday morning. Snow has settled all across the bay wherever there's no incoming tide channels. It's on all the windward sides of tree boles and in the clear parts of the woodland where I'm standing, west of the burn that flows into Sailean an Eorna. The trunks themselves are patchworked by mosses and snow drift, set against off white lichens with here and there a snuff coloured lichen on nearby rocks. Lungworts (Lobaria pulmonaria), also on the trunks, are a leathery green, vaguely lizard like. This is mature oakwood, with a few fallen trees, sparse and interspersed with holly and hazel. There's a few birch trees here too. The fallen trees are almost certainly a result of storms, perhaps hurricanes. Some are split, the weight of large branches become insupportable in high wind, while others are toppled entire, with rootplates at right angles to the woodland floor, though it's seldom horizontal on this slope leading down to the loch.

One fallen limb, a metre round, is eighteen paces long, from the main trunk, but still joined; it's a sessile oak; the main trunk a metre and a half round. Growth has been good from this limb, curving up and away from it, its recurving forms giving living space to a variety of epiphytes.

The oaks here have a massive beauty, fallen or standing, their relic lives entwined with each other and with all the other species of the woodland. Here, in a rootplate ten feet high (more than three metres) growing straight up, while the oak shoots from its recline, is a holly. It's more than double my handspan round, the displayed upper roots all elbows and knuckles smooth as if polished. From the same plate is one of the ubiquitous birches, though smaller than the holly. Another oak, standing, has a massively thickened lower trunk, made that way by epicormic growth. Its girth is more than five metres round. Lying close by is another ancient of four metres' girth with a partner birch, older this time, maybe a metre and a half round. The bole of the fallen oak is host, under the snow, to a small holly, showing only its first pair of true leaves – last year's germination. Its roots will grow and assist the oak's subsidence back into the soil and rock from which it slowly rose. The ivies run round straight trunks, which subdivide fairly low into main branches. Each subsequent division curves and curves again, some so much they seem to spiral on themselves, sometimes almost making knots.

I try to read the woodland, limb by limb and leaf after leaf. Its full story is conjecture. The epiphytes are an indication of ancient woodland, but it will have been worked here too, coppiced, perhaps, certainly bark stripping happened, and selective felling for charcoal. There may have also been plantings; though now there's no indication of this. The woodland, like all worked landscape, is art, and as such, fictive. If I'm expounding on the great book of the woodland, the lives of the trees, their history and economics, then each tree, in its subdividing and recurving limbs, is reciting genetics, performing climate and topography, geology and its own personal survival so far.

My ignorance is boundless. Not only can I not know the trees' stories, the woodland itself reaches beyond history. I can't tell the names of the mosses and lichens. But I'm happy in my lack of knowledge; nothing at all can stop me from fully experiencing the setting and enjoying the secrecy of the trees; their utter stillness, which nevertheless they impart to me, here for a short while.

As I leave the oaks, just two feet from where I pass, and not at all bothered, a huffed up goldcrest is bobbing and pushing her head into snowdrifts, below which are small plants' seedheads which she raids in her search for warmth.

4th

In the flat grey and foreshortening light, it's hard to see the hinds, unless they move. Although I know they are there, if they're still, and they usually are, then with the naked eye, even their white rear flashes can be mistaken for lichen on a rock. Their faded rust coloured broken coats are entirely the complexion of the winter bracken, broken down as it is by wind, and curling that way and this after a season's rain.

The three hinds of this quarter, though, have been joined by another three. There's no stand-off, none of the stags' confrontational bellow. It's more irritation on the part of the original trio; they move on ahead, grazing, browsing, moving further up the hill with flicks of the heads and eyes and ears as the others make small transgressions into the precise margins of sociability.

The same bounds apply to all the gregarious animals here. The cormorants on the rock beyond Eilean Dubh are absolutely evenly spaced. If one lands on the rock, having fished awhile, the whole colony must needs shuffle sideways to allow her in, but without breaking the pattern of spacing. The chaffinches bustle about fallen seeds, but keep within the same imperative limits.

There's food enough for them all, and no need of overcrowding and jostling. I'm mindful of this, brought back to the Byre by thirst, as I make the first morning pot of tea for one.

6th

With heavy rain alternating with longer pauses from rain, insubstantial mist hovers over forestry and woodland alike. It rolls over rockfaces and slowly topples downhill. It's hard not to see Chinese landscape scrolls in this as I walk along: pines, rock, water and mist unfolding; now obscured by brief abundant showers, here clearing to reveal a mossy worty oak. The ropes and tresses of the hills' overburdens of water from a distance make their sinuous white way to the loch; up close, they fall sheer and bounce fiercely from boulder to outcrop in torrents and surges that would wash stags away.

The hinds of the bog pick their usual way west, with perhaps a little more elegant high stepping than usual; the wet ground, no doubt. Their three followers seem to have deserted them; maybe they were passing through, looking for their own territory.

Apart from the deer, there's only a grey crow, on the road verge, moving with that odd sort of sidle strut that suggests stilt walking. Overhead, now the rain's off for a while, just two ravens. They're very low, negotiating the coast down on cool air, close enough for whiffling wing sounds to be heard. Their muted, offhand, gamelan calls to each other fold me in to another temporality. I pause; the birds hang in sky; then it's movement again.

9th

gamb'yan gamb'yan
our dream
colour of dawn
our song
gamb'yan gamb'yan

gyawalot'gyawalot'gyawa-lolololoi(t)
gyawalot'gyawalot'gyawa-lolololoi(t)
gyawalot'gyawalot'gyawa-lolololoi(t)
gyawalot'gyawalot'gyawa-lolololoi(t)
gyawalot'gyawalot'gyawa-lolololoi(t)

is part of Shimpei Kusano's wild but tender rendition of frogs' voices in his poem *Birthday Party*.

With a paring of the storm moon high in the true blue sky, the day is clear for anything. Frogs have already found that clarity and a breath of spring for their clutching and spawning in the ditches. When they disappear again, they leave behind hundreds of eggs, each in a ball of jelly as proof of their passion. Or imperative genes. Amplexus is the clasp of a male on a female's back; an embracing kind of copulation where the male fertilises the female's eggs as they emerge into the water. The poet Shimpei Kusano, for whom frogs were a metaphor of life itself, had no doubt: genes and libido are one and the same, driving frogs; all living things. In an echo of the swelling moon, these eggs will grow to become tadpoles by the time of the last quarter of this moon. Each globe of jelly holds the beginning of a frog, a black speck far smaller than the head of a safety match.

Once I had an ancient glass battery jar and watched this development in the cold porch each year, never tiring of the astonishment of spring childhood, of the dream of life becoming. Now, I'm content to watch as I pass the shallow wild water. The frogs have sung their soft songs. To slightly paraphrase Shimpei Kusano in his epilogue to Birthday Party: *"as author I have no desire to stop the choir at this party celebrating birth. by a ditch near the burn at Gobsheallach, by Acharacle, in the peninsula of Ardnamurchan in the western Highlands. a party of points tinier than sesame seed as yet. this ecstasy's swaying echoing flowing place."*

A new spring and I step along the path together.

11th

After another clear sky day, the moon has set and above me is an ocean-field of stars of all magnitudes. Even this third night of dark-walking, how little I trust my senses. Trying to abandon hesitancy and step out, since I know the paths, I stumble over every pebble, wonder at the nearness of rock and tree trunk. Soon, however, eyes accustom themselves to starlight and I'm aware of other things at the edges of perception – the squeaking in the ditch, which would suggest a small rodent unwisely voicing at my footfall; something that could be the slightest of draughts from a passing wing; I'm straining towards physical understanding of this blackly transformed landscape.

After the unaccustomed brilliance of the day where all has been psychotropically bright, especially the trunks of these silent white birches, walking with no light but the boundlessness of stars is moving from dream to dream. In all the runnels and burns is a sparkling from the light of centuries past sent by distant luminous gas to enliven water.

Night birds sing. I can only look up; I'm stopped and still, mind silenced by light. Starlight that's veering here and there into the red and green parts of the spectrum as those gaseous masses pulse like the throb of blood in my brain, lighting my eyes.

There is no scale for this except, as ever, that of my own body. and its untrusted senses. I touch the mosses, I smell the drying soon-spring earth, I hear the whirr of a snipe as she plummets downhill; tonight, mortality has a metallic taste at the back of the bared throat. But it's sight that's rubric for imagination, allowing through these pupils untold immensities of light. Of light which is a greed and a curiosity for every corner of life.

14th

valentine

you are not here
walked by retreating tide uprooted oarweed has left an arcing trail one
hundred and ninety four paces long
sand's mirror of the crescent moon's camber across kingfisher sky
sun cast water shadow ripples and bubbles on
ridges of sand the ebb moves across
surface coruscating with brilliance
oak leaves flattened along sand edge
oystercatcher imprints
Tornado jet contrail
thirty five curlews plainsong wheel and silver into that white
lichened anticline and syncline rising straight from the seabed
the print of hinds' feet on the foreshore
a herring gull sings
heron and grey crow make refrain

where do the sea paths lead
where do the boulevards of cold sky lead
and the heart's trance

looping and winding each other
as sound follows ear
as sea follows eye
as the heron invents us all through the flat shine of the tidal pool
you are the lichen inspector
you listen when the mussel beds crackle
you grade the ocean's weeds
kelp and bladderwrack
you measure the frost inching up the oak bole
you speak to the troubled wren
and I'm islanded here where
you are vein and artery

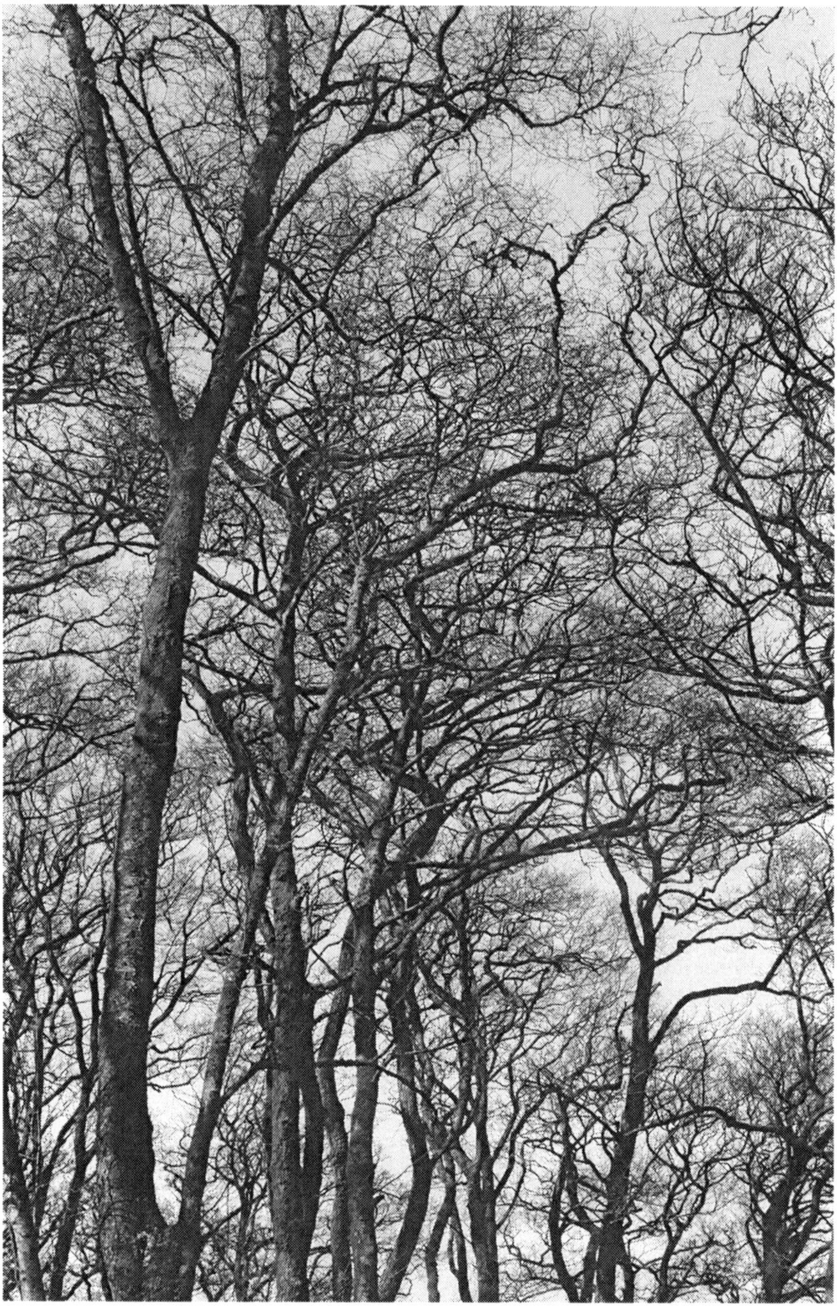

15th

The thing is, we get the point more quickly when we realize it is we looking rather than that we may not be seeing it.
    John Cage: Lecture on Nothing

you who hurry toward leviathan woods,
you who walk into the gloom of clouds and mountains,
fasten up your raincoat, damn it.
    Miyazawa Kenji: Traveler

Although I consider the soaring eagle to be a good omen for the day, I'm kept grounded myself by Miyazawa's words as I make off up the hill from the loch. Even after noon, as this is, there's pockets where that frost painting of bracken – a silvering outline of each brown dead frond – is evident, along with the woodland floor's resistant crunch as I walk.

 It's axiomatic that if you go looking for the woodlands they're not there; just the trees. Once you've given up looking (and a lifetime is too short) then you arrive. Here, against the backdrop of the loch, with split rocks from which moss'd ferned birch and oak spring up like woody fountains; among litters of lichened twigs, broken from boughs by storms, it's easy to get caught up in the detail of the trees. Individuals: oaks with their leaders neatly snapped by gales, long fallen limbs debarked, each showing twists of growth round on itself; a triple stemmed ancient sheltering a holly. Out of the burn's gorge rise hazels all keeled at ninety degrees to the slope, rising at right angles to that growth and bifurcating, a metre round, mossy, stretching for the light away from the always shade of the gorge. An ivy winds round a young oak, with its choking climb upward. There's triple-stemmed oaks, double-stemmed oaks, rarely a straight singleton stem.

 Slowly, I realise, as I follow deer tracks through all this, brushing spiderwebs from my face, that there are open spaces in the canopy (even though the leaves are still only buds, the twigging above can be dense) and that in fact, I am indeed looking at a sort of parkland or savannah brought about by intermittent grazing. I'm seeing the woodland. I give a little shake, moving with the dance of gnats in the afternoon sun in one such opening; I notice the flitter of small fragile-as-dust buff coloured moths. And there: even a red admiral butterfly fresh from hibernation, with its erratic zigzagging flight.

Among the oaks in this are hollies, which may or may not have started as infill among them. Sometimes hollies may predate oaks. Just on a small rise is a quartet of old fellows among the heather and fraughàn, bracken and ubiquitous moss, rising to ten feet up the oak boles; higher up are small ferns, perhaps the hard fern, Blechnum spicant (though my ignorance extends to ferns as well). These old hollies are almost within touch of each other; one's a five stem with a stem dead, the next has three stems with two dead, the remaining two have healthy twin stems. It's not clear whether this is because the trees were coppiced at one time. They're like broken toothed oldsters anywhere, sharing a rueful joke at the expense of youngsters around them. At their swollen bases is another indicator of spring coming from below: tender fresh leaves of wood sorrel, which is truly delicious and less vinegary now than at any other time throughout the year.

Birch and oak are indiscriminate in sheltering, here and there, juvenile sitka spruces, their seeds carried by wind and squirrel from the forestry plantation to the west. A small winged creature lands on my hand as I lean contemplating the mossy decomposing lines of trunks and rootplates. A dead oak takes at least a century to disappear completely, so these must have fallen at least fifty years ago, though the moss blanketing may have speeded up decomposition by a few years. There's a young oak, maybe fifty years old, liberated into the light by the fall of these prostrate forms, perhaps; but like any crone, bent backed, growing three feet up, then at right angles to that, then straight up again. In the hummocks and tussocks of sphagnums (how I've tried to identify them; always I come back to: it's a sphagnum, never further) there are birches sloughing their skins like any adder, along the lines of dead limbs all the way down to the floor. Moss seals and heals the lowest cracks; other birch branches from the same trunks are vibrant with new growth buds. The dead limbs, stripped of bark demonstrate clearly the twists of slow spiralling plants following sun clockwise. Scabs of lichen everywhere. Growth in, around and on everything, sap driven, moss softened, rain nourished. As many dead as living; as many wounded as healthy. A slow war of attrition with weather, browsing and life itself, even, especially, in February, bristling crawling and packed brimful on the woodland slope.

I walk and walk in pasture-woodland's own reverie, until the sky is streaked with cirrostratus over the eggblue of morning and noon gone and the sun moves toward a Morvern evening to the west. There's the rumble of high flying unseen jets; gossamer catches the low light finding its way under the heavy limbs. Oakwoods found and lost. I've been looking and seeing all along.

16th

What shall be given unto thee? or what shall be done unto thee, thou false tongue?
Sharp arrows of the mighty, with coals of juniper.
Psalm 102

Juniper burns very hot, without smoke, maybe that's why it was used in the whisky stills in the hills; no betraying smoke for the Revenue men to spot. Alastair Cameron tells the story of two other Camerons, Donald and Hugh, their ponies laden with whisky, who met a gauger for the Revenue at a river. "He did not reveal his identity, neither did they express any sign of suspicion." "As there was a good flow of water", Donald offered to carry the gauger across the river on his back, to save him from getting wet. The Revenue man agreed, but when in mid stream, Donald flung him into it, yelling to Hugh to give stick to the ponies and "take to your heels, son of John, son of Hugh."

It's only ten or eleven miles from here that happened. I leave the new road, a highway for these parts, and backtrack a little onto the old road, leaving it immediately to cross Abhainn Coire an Iubhair, the river of the yew corrie, which runs, flatly at this point through a stone bed in something approaching ox-bows, north to south. The river is fed by so many small tributary burns that they have no names. To the west, curving round to the north is the corrie, a cauldron, a blind glen, with its head turned back on itself by Beinn Bheag. Here lies the actual cauldron, a lochan surrounded by twisted contours and contorted outcrops and upthrusts, all worn to a smoothness, save for where they've been more recently cracked by frosts. From here down to the sea loch, it's steep-sided, a classic glacier scour. Along the river bed at this level, not far above the sea, the banks are lined with holly. With alder, which it outnumbers, it's the only tree here. The dead spate-borne grass stalks are three feet up the trunks, showing the rough and tumble of the winter rains and snow melt, though all week it's been dry and the river soon drops. Heading north and up, with the corrie sides enclosing now, the hollies peter out.

Nothing but heather. To the east the ridge, Druim an Iubhair, becomes more pronounced. Iubhair, yew, in this instance as with most other place-names containing it, does not refer to yew, but to mountain-yew, *iubhair-beinne* as Carmichael had it from Eoghan Wilson in the Blessing of the Struan, *iubhair-creige* elsewhere. Juniper. And, at the turning west of the whole corrie, but on the low ridge to the east, it's lowly growing.

In the nineteenth century, it was so common here that sacks of berries were sent to market in Inverness and Aberdeen, where they were bought by merchants to send to Holland to make their gin, jenever. Juniper and jenever are cognate, from the Latin *juniperus*, which is its genus name, communis being the specific; but the procumbent form of these beautiful conifers, one of three native here, clinging like a waterfall to the rocks from which it cascades, is the subspecies *nana (syn. sibirica, alpina)*. This plant, to thrive, needs a certain lack of competition from heathers and grasses when seeds set; a controlled grazing provides that; but latterly the glens and corries have suffered from the sheep and are very much overgrazed, meaning the sheep (and deer) will eat the seedlings as soon as they appear. The fact that this has happened for more than one generation means that all the juniper is old and making little, if any seed. The future may hold only extinction; like the yew itself, juniper might only be found in captivity – churchyards, botanic gardens.

Which all adds to the quick joy of finding plants here, some with their flowing trunks as thick as my forearm; a pleasure only to be found by prolonged looking, sometimes in the bitter cold, as today. The scramble up a ridge, slick with seeping water, finger and toe-holds carefully sought, bringing a soft green, light to dark, slightly pricky-leaved plant up close, to caress, is to come to terms with the Gaelic name and to breathe in the plant. Mountain yew it certainly is. A true psalm zinging in bare rock, livening the whole corrie with its ancient presence.

I once spent an entire day at Taynish searching for these plants (though not the dwarf subspecies found here) without success (albeit with the consolation of chanterelles). As well as the overgrazing, maybe the illicit stills in the glens and hills helped the depletion to the point where I rejoice to see a couple of plants; where before it was plentiful enough to lend its name to river, corrie and ridge. Maybe the psalm is lament.

As it is, I toast the survivors with Waterford sloes potently and redly infusing Cork gin, a birthday gift made by Morven. My own small shebeen back at the Byre, with the shade of Donald Cameron.

18th

3 events at Gobsheallach today

This morning, a column of cloud rises from Bein Resipol, from just below the summit into the upper sky. Volcanoes look like this.

At noon, a grey crow flies down to the large sheet of unleavened bread, stale and curling, that I've put out front of the byre for her. With claw and beak, she neatly quarters it and flaps away with the whole bread in her beak.

An eagle eats up the miles westward with an easy but fast flight. She is silhouetted for a moment against a pale moon, three days away from full.

25th

On the ruddy golden coat of the warrantable deer the bright sunlight shone, so that the colour seemed unsteady, or as if it was visibly emanating and flowing forth in undulations.
                    Richard Jefferies; *Red Deer*

Having only yesterday performed the comedy classic of falling off a ladder, I'm hirpling about among the trees and in no position to go chasing over the heather and moss after the white red deer stag that's been sighted in the west highlands. If white red deer stag sounds like tautology, not to mention contradictory, that's what the animal himself is. Of course, he has no idea (I guess) that he is in any way exceptional.

What makes him special is that he is leucistic. Leucism is a reduction of all types of skin pigmentation, resulting in a white skin or coat, unlike albinism, which is a reduction of melanin only. Leucistic animals have normally pigmented eyes. Leucism is also seen in the irregular patches on other animals – the hides of some cattle, where localized hypopigmentation gives the pied effect in differing patterns of Friesian herds, for example.

For me, that's enough, but white stags have always exerted a kind of reverse shadow on the imagination. There's lots of talk about the special nature of such a stag. Those who see him are sure (it's said) to have a profound change imminent in their lives. A white stag also seems to have been conflated into a unicorn in past ages. Now we're perhaps a trifle more materialistic; though Latter Day Shamans, Druids, and Wicca folk were outraged by the shooting and decapitation of a white stag last autumn on Exmoor, presumably as a trophy for sale. These folk, and to be fair, many others, including local farmers, not normally given to vapours of a mystical kind, spoke of the sacred nature of the animal. What they all feel on the shooting and beheading of red red deer stags is not recorded.

The red deer in Scotland, indigenous to these parts, is too often seen as an opportunity; a resource. Whether for venison or the thrill of stalking with a camera, it raises so many questions, from landownership to local food sourcing, from woodland regeneration to wolf reintroduction, that I'm actually pleased not to be in any fit condition to bother the white one by walking in his area (I know his whereabouts): he doesn't need me ogling him as a curiosity. His peers, the other stags, have no doubts that he's one of them and another rival come rutting time. No more, no less.

I'm not much for walking anyway. Walking for me in the past usually had a purpose, like helping gather sheep, or walking to the hay meadow. Sitting still, contemplating the way the sun moves, or the tide comes and goes and to see what the woods, waters and fields bring my way has never been a problem though.

This year, I've been re-examining that attitude; spending time walking the woodlands in what Richard Holloway calls "exuberant purposelessness". I have no purpose, other than to observe the poetry of clouds and winds; to cheer the dance of gnats and moths, to listen intently to the musical compositions of wrens and herring gulls. There's no point to caressing the moss as I go, to saluting the ancient oaks; no point to commiserating with the birch on the loss of its limb. But I do it all anyway. It's for no reason I study for half an hour the spider spinning a filament across my path, then walking round it. I have nothing in mind when I see the rising and wheeling of herons over Garbh Eilean and count them to be, today, nineteen in number. The woodlands are full, if not of purpose, then of clarity and movement. Each creature here has enough intent for me as well. Exuberance rises from the knowledge that I am not needed. The woodlands are as liberating of egotism as of ideas and objectives.

I have no need to follow unicorns.

27th

The moon is sliding the sea into its tidal heaping back into the bay again.

How tender the hill is where the woodlands are thin; a child with solitary promise. Spring is here, whatever the weather, and it has been wild and wet, but mild with it. The colonies of birch with their hair-like traceries of twigs have small ochre leafbuds and are putting out their first catkins. Spring's not reluctant, but I'm happy still to be in the bareness of the woods, finding great pleasure in the journey; enjoying the forms of the trees and their limbs, boughs, branches and twigs rising towards the increased light of advancing days. Unless it's possible to appreciate the underlying structure of winter's austerity, then surely it would be hard to welcome the leaf, blossom and fruit of summer. I'm reminded here of just how much like purple figs alder buds are, just at the point of ripening; it's a matter of scale. The hazels have extended their lime green catkins; every branchlet terminates with a small club shaped bud. The contorted willows (weather does this, it's not a true contorted form) have tiny rufous buds. Each fragile brittle length of woodbine ends with six newly opened leaves, while amid the tangle, in the sheltered hollows where burns roll to the sea, the first handsbreadth blades of flag iris thrust their sword leaves through rust brown rot from clearly visible rhizomes. The furze has been flowering a month and more, its almond scented yellow a discussion of dormancy with the iris, which will not show colour for a full two months yet. There's a rippling cloud in every transient puddle; the newly minted translucency of holly leaves glows against the dark green waxyness of the old sharp foliage. The little faint buds of the dog rose call the pink-white flowers that'll rise from stems. Aspens, still now, have heavy pointed chocolate coloured buds, which will soon start their wind whispering as leaves. Out at sea a curlew's ringing its song. And the oaks – all ages leaning into the hill, woven with ivies, sheltering holly and birch saplings, their every branch-end knobbled and swelling, last year's lobed and brown papery leaves still clinging, the mossy oaks are distending their strong pointed buff and sandy buds. Everything's bubbling and fizzing its irresistible course through trunk and stem, through sap, bud and blood. On the rocks, lichens continue their concentric growth like soft moist meandering trails of night-time snails.

There's a convocation of crows in a half mile circle around me, from rock to outermost tree top; they bow and sing rasping beautiful songs and no-one to hear; no-one to see their spanning but the seven hinds of Airigh Bheagaig, eyebright and long soft leather ears pricked, and a solitary sceptical buzzard hunched in her own glamour.

I'm back at the Byre just as the sulphur coloured evening rain begins its downpour, lashing bud and me and the incoming sea alike.

March
3rd

> *wearing a summer hat.*
> *walked out into powdery snow.*
>   Shimpei Kusano: Certain Days

Leap Year's day came and went. The smallest hind of Gobsheallach hill has not been seen for five days; in her place is a small stag, timid and keeping close to the two larger hinds as they move across the bay, exposed, and as they browse on the sparse green among rusting bracken. Has the small hind been shot, or is there some transformation happening here in this corner of a materialistic land where a white stag can be explained by leucism?

I'm content here, heaping language onto landscape, through winter's mouldering, now watching spring's shoots; but I'm leaving Ardnamurchan, on a day of blizzards alternating with the blue-blindness of cloud-free skies. The dramas of the mountains, companionable Beinn Resipol and Beinn Hianta in Morvern and the doings of the waters: Loch Shiel, Loch Sunart, and Abhainn an Iubhair and the burns and puddles no longer ask my daily attention. Spring is a good time to leave; though I will still be writing, more slowly, of the walking of last summer, last spring, grounded in memory and experience. The Atlantic wind will blow my nose cold from another quarter. Like any trumpeting swan I'm migrating; like any wild goose, I'll land again on this bog, unworked since the sixties, near Airigh Bheagaig.

What's left is poetry.

17th

Camas Torsa

glacier talks
under ocean moon

above Resipole rises and shrinks
tide swills and hangs

Spindrift's gutting across
sun's line of gulls

its engine throb hub
of the scoured world

April
3rd

this is not an explanation or critique of Camas Torsa, but another poem, titled

COMMENTARY

we construct landscape
as identity
there is no water imagine
imagine there is no sea loch
Resipole has its foundation
in syncline
cormorant curves in
that nothing which is something
already easing away
the mountain's walking off
into that hour before
dawn that is the same every
where everywhere

23rd

Sailean nan Cuileag

the pelt of sea its tongues
smooring and quenching and

plucking what will be left
at tide's going air

of what's uttered oystercatcher's
pitch and pipe smew and craik of

curlew pulse of what's given
what's yielded what's opened

June
19th

Ceann Tràigh Breige

tender flesh to sit
foolish and hoping

to be
come mountain

the sun bides in
the loch surfacing

cormorants can't
look in its void eye

Port na h-Uamha

sea's scales
grey crow rises straight

from rock to
plummet crack

cockles and her
self falls

south wind riffs
a blue line pulleys up oak

Garbh Eilean

cold fingertips
legacy of the quick

ocean drools on
otter's back

on hooping-under
cormorant

body catching up
arriving

Sàilean an Eòrna

o there's
nothing but

Resipole being
mountain

here
on its

fund in
sea

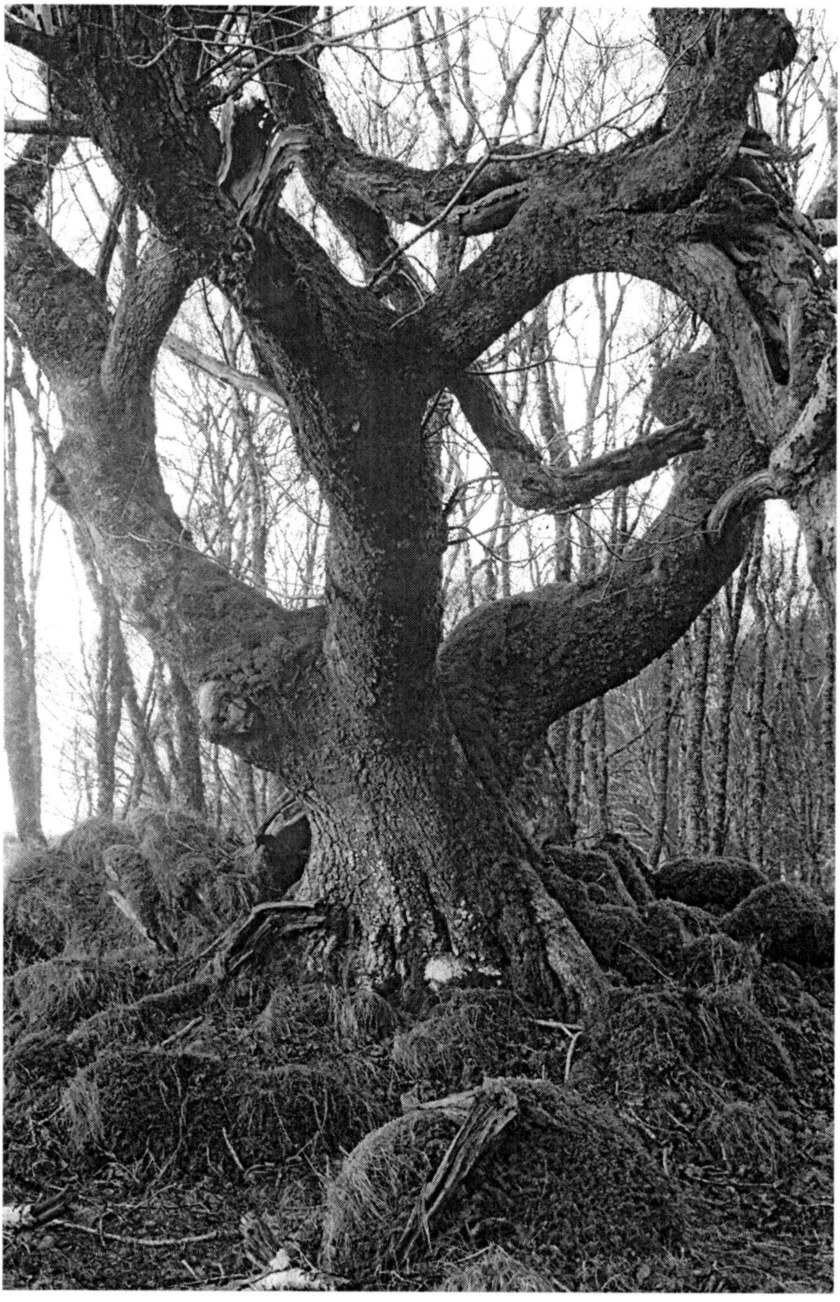

2
Saari

Sunday, 5 September 2010
At home

Bittersweet, harebells and yarrow. By the bay in the mixed woodland there are anthills: three feet high and maybe eight feet in diameter. The ants are moving relatively slowly after a hot summer of intense activity. Cooling off a little. I feel at home here at once; with familiar friends, though I'm still jinkin, deliberately not yet visiting the little oakwood of Tammimäke.

Instead I'm mooching by the sea along the side of Mietoistenlahti, the innermost inlet of Mynälahti Bay, which leads to Saarenaukko. Unravelling place names is a difficult business. Aukko is given in my little Finnish dictionary as a gap or opening; but I'll leave that alone until I can ask a Finn. It's certainly an opening though, salt water inland. If I were to thread my way south-west through uncountable islands and skerries of the Turku archipelago, I'd reach the Baltic. Northwest, I'd come into the Gulf of Bothnia: but I have no boat or charts; instead I'm ambling along the shore of the bay, past the herd of Aberdeen Angus cattle and over the electric fence.

The woodland here is made up of rowan, Scots pine, spruces. Birch of course, but also alder with its feet wet as ever; the fine surprise for me is the large number of juniper trees. All these seem to be slightly rimed with salt and I can feel it on the wind. There's a red squirrel, which I took to be a bracket fungus of some sort at first, looking down on me. Its tail curved along its back, calmly, unmoving, it surveys me– a curious intruder in this place. I've no strong liquor yet to use the juniper berries, nor can I think how to dry them for cooking, but I can't forbear picking these rowanberries – bright red under the thinnest of salt coatings. It'll make fine jelly with maybe a tang of the Baltic sea to counter its sweetness. The trees grow among lichen covered rock outcrops, spreading their limbs along contours, rooting into crannies. These are the trees I want berries from, not their more upright cousins a little inland. There's always a more intense flavour from anything which grows in the adversity of wind and weather. I get great pleasure from the ripping sound as I comb the berry clusters on the branches through my fingers direct into my bag. I'll come back for the juniper berries, as well as the ripe fraochan – blaeberries – fruiting from thin soil on the fringes of the bedrock.

Geese are wheeling noisily overhead in their dozens, breasting the wind a moment then beating up against it before falling to the salt marsh: a whole tribe of Daedalus folk. I come across a small boathouse or rather fishermen's hut hard by an inlet just big enough for a half dozen boats. They all look a little neglected; the most interesting among them a wooden clinker-built snub nosed dinghy, its bright blue paint peeling, its belly full of water. From the hut hangs a plastic northern shoveller duck decoy, a summer visitor here, as well as some hoops and half hoops across which are stretched fishing nets. Here also are a couple of abandoned ice sledges, one with a fine orange painted kitchen-style wooden chair straddling the wooden braces above the runners. There's also the usual remains of a couple of rotting wooden boats and oddly, a double seater swing in a frame. Maybe the old fishermen enjoyed a smoke after a day's haul, swinging gently in summer breezes.

I walk back with my full bag over my shoulder along the unmetalled road. A farmer is tedding – two rows into one high windrow. The crop seems herb rich and will make fine fodder, maybe for the Angus cattle over by the bay. We wave as we pass each other. There's some late swallows skimming as low across the cut-over meadows as the geese were high. The insects that lived in the fields they hunted are gone; just stubble. In the slanting evening sun a snake is basking on the dirt of the road. It's probably a grass snake, though seems to have unusual colour configurations: unmarked along its rippling spine and with distinct black and white head bands. I touch it gently and suggest it moves – the tractor will soon pass this way – but it simply flickers its tongue at me. I'm persistent with my explaining tongue and right forefinger and it gives up and winds its way quickly on its scaly belly into the undergrowth at the roadside.

The ash trees hang branches heavy with seed; dust is blowing across the field after the farmer's tedding wheels. There's a change in the air; the gathering in of summer. Hay rich with camomile and fleabane. Bittersweet.

Monday, 6 September 2010
Scaup and smew

There's a gentle rasping of oak limbs one against another in the north wind. It stopped me where I was carefully walking, thinking I'd heard a very dainty woodpecker.

On the fringes of the little oakwood Tammimäki are birches and some poplar, but here at the centre is very little but oak, just a small number of rowans. Oak of all ages, from the oldest, which I measure tip of nose to outstretched left fingertips as one yard, to be five yards in circumference to the smallest underfoot saplings, a single stem and inches high. There's little or no grazing here so the regeneration is thick, healthy and vibrant.

Among the freestanding large boulders the woodland floor is carpeted with berries. Down low, the lily of the valley berries glow orange, poisonous miniature persimmons. Herb Paris too, its single fruited stem offering what appears to be a cultivated blueberry. It's a narcotic. Mrs Grieve tells me it's only used in homeopathy these days, and considered poisonous. There's a red berry borne by a plant with leaves like a raspberry but growing low. The only edible berry here is the wild redcurrant, growing higher, but just about tasteless.

It's a small woodland, cared for by the government: conserved with minimal management. I see dead trees left to stand or fall as they will. There's also some that have been deliberately ring-barked: a double cut deep into the wood that killed these trees which were certainly alien species. But in decay and death they have provided homes for more invertebrates than they did alive.

They are still standing and I'm thinking of the old gamekeepers' gibbets on which were hung "vermin": unwanted species around a pheasant run – crows, foxes, buzzards and the like. Our manipulation of other species is unbounded.

I don't think anyone walks here any more, but there's the remains of a stone dyke, more of a boundary marker made from large boulders removed from the adjacent field, than anything to keep stock in or out. It's hard to get to grips with the origins of this woodland. Most Finnish woods are of mixed trees – predominantly birch and pine. A complete stand of oaks, extending to a woodland is rare.

A brown dragonfly moves along the path ahead of me as I leave Tammimäki and head west for the wetlands which are a staging post for birds on their migrations. The beautifully named garganey and gadwall, the scaup and smew all rest here. As do some thousand of greylag geese who are here at the moment, until their long flight south and west to Spain.

And dancing, circling cranes.

The geese ululate and warble above; resting in a form is what seems to be a hare in the middle of the big cutover wheatfield next to the bay. As I move south, inland a little through a deep fringe of woods, aspens are rattling in the wind and a little below that red squirrels are dancing, making curious soft clicking noises. Now and then a leaf falls from their gymnastic browsing and flutters slowly to the floor of the wood. There's a drone of winged insects. The wood is an orchestra this evening – from the aeolian harp top notes, to the cello continuo of mosquitoes.

I've done a kind of spontaneously choreographed walk here, led by sightings – now under this tree, now against that bank – of mushrooms; led as much by my appetite as any squirrel.

I head for home with the sun beginning to sink, a bagful of what Finns call butter ceps – sticky and brown on top, butter yellow underneath.

Tuesday, 7 September 2010
St Patrick

At the very same spot that a couple of days ago I persuaded the grass snake to quit the unmetalled sandy road, this morning on my way down to the shoreline, there's a dead adder. It's at a point near a barn on a slight rise where the sun strikes hot – or as hot as it gets in September in Finland, which this year is fairly hot: 19 degrees today. On the sand, an obvious place for reptiles to bask. When I pick it up, it reaches from the ground almost to my waist. It's roadkill, though nothing will eat it but scavenging beetles and other insects. The poor beast's intestines are coiled out; blackened blood coating them with around that, a grime of sandy soil. I examine the head and teeth with care, noting the grin of death, and then stretch the dead snake out to rest in the cool grass. It was a big male, as thick as a child's wrist, with a zig of black lightning all along its spine.

Having tired of the conversation of geese – it's all one sided – they never listen – I head for home and here at this same wee rise in the road is an adder. A strong male again, guts erupting. Thinking it's the one of the morning, I check anyway; but there's that one I laid in the grass still unmoving, dead. I retrace my few steps, noticing blood staining the dirt and examine the second one. He has a yellow underpart to his tail. As I lift him to measure and heft, he writhes gently and I realise he's still alive. It's hard to know what to do – I don't kill things. Is the viper suffering? I lay him in the grass like the first and at this point I notice the small nick on my pinky – bleeding gently. My brain tells me that a dead adder and a half dead one don't bite and I'm sure I was careful to keep my fingers away from fangs, but I suck the knuckle and spit anyway, an atavistic but maybe prudent reaction.

Having finished work for the day, and since it's still early – light and warm, I ramble down to visit the geese again. I'm ever hopeful of engaging them in a short discourse. My two adders are still there, the second cold now; basking between the two corpses, on the dirt road in the last of the day's heat is a female adder. I have no truck with anthropomorphism but nevertheless it's hard not to wonder: why a female? Why now and why between two dead males. I know the logical explanations.

I pluck a long stem of rosebay willow herb with its seeds still adhering, to persuade her to leave the road. This is all getting a little biblical. I'm feeling like some latter day saint (not a Mormon, that would be odd) but a sort of Patrick, banishing snakes from a dirt track in Mynämäki. The snake bares her fangs and raises her head to strike as I gently brush. A long moment passes then we both retire: she to the long grass gracefully, me a step backwards with none of the grace of either saint or snake.

Thursday, 9 September 2010
Oak and maple

Trees are being planted at Saari Manor. Oaks and maples, puddled in well to this sandy soil. There's been no rain for days. The green rain gauge by the barn is empty; dry on its iron cradle. The young trees are well tended, broken roots trimmed back along with damaged branches, but nothing else – the curve of young limbs as they've formed where they first were grown are left to find their own way to the light in this new home.

There's harmony in the planting of trees. A music of hole digging and root pruning, of puddling and planting; of hands on the roots to spread and gently bury them; the tamping and raking and setting aside of stones.

And there's songs in the tools used and laid by in casual lunchtime arrangements: the blue-back handle of the bow saw with its black blade lever and the two orange-handled loppers, one short and the other long, against an ash stem; the blue-shafted spade with its yellow handle (a more spoonlike spade than mine at home) together with the orange-toothed soft rake and the black steel rake against an old oak. And over there, stabbed in the turf, an isolated spade.

Greylags

I spend my days mostly in silence, around the little oakwood or at the shoreline. It's been years since I smoked a cigarette, but I can still feel that intake of smoke past the lips and down. A dram would be good, though maybe at midday, whisky – even a good Islay – would prevent much fruitful thinking – since that's what I'm attempting. But looking out over the bay, these stimulants might just be a substitute for speech. Or thought.

The greylag geese resolutely refuse to answer me, so I simply listen to their conversations. I can't understand the fine points of their humour, though they do laugh a lot, but the gist of the grammar seems clear enough – it's based on volume. The louder the language (or maybe it's a dialect; is greylag a variation on beangoose or Canada goose?) the more they are likely to take flight. Softer whiffles and gurgles denote contentment. So much is universal. The orthography of their language is beyond me mostly though. There are vocables that have no exact equivalent in English. Finnish might come closer, with its vowel and consonant clusters. But the most tricky would be that *click* which humans can only make at the back of the throat – and then not all of us.

Individual greylags make words: ***eu ö***; **k'-eu k'o**; and phrases: **eu ö k'eu eu eu; wy, eu ö-ö-ö** on a rising inflection. And then with that near back of throat click: **wee – 'k' ö wa'k' yeu yeu yeu.**

What I do understand is when they rise up in cackles and hoots and barks, wheeling higher and round again, their cries collectively mingle: they become one organism with one voice: a distant gale howling when the cabin door is shut and the fire's lit.

Friday, 10 September 2010
Conversation

I'm standing with my hands in my pockets by the side of the road. I'm contemplating the stones beneath the oaks. They are not small, but each maybe the size of a kitchen chair and have been dropped off here from the front loader of a tractor at some time I'm guessing. There's an odd thing here with age. These oaks have been here a long time – from the girth of the largest I've seen, 250 years at a guess. Who knows what generations preceded them. I'll try to find out the history of this little wood as I can, but for now, I'm thinking at least 250 years.

They're growing on thin sandy soil; bedrock emerges here and there, covered with plumages of lichen and short mosses. The oaks have an intimate relation with the rock and the soil. The new kitchen chair rocks are just as old as the bedrock – they were perhaps left behind in Mynämäki by a retreating glacier; rubble, but the stuff of geology.

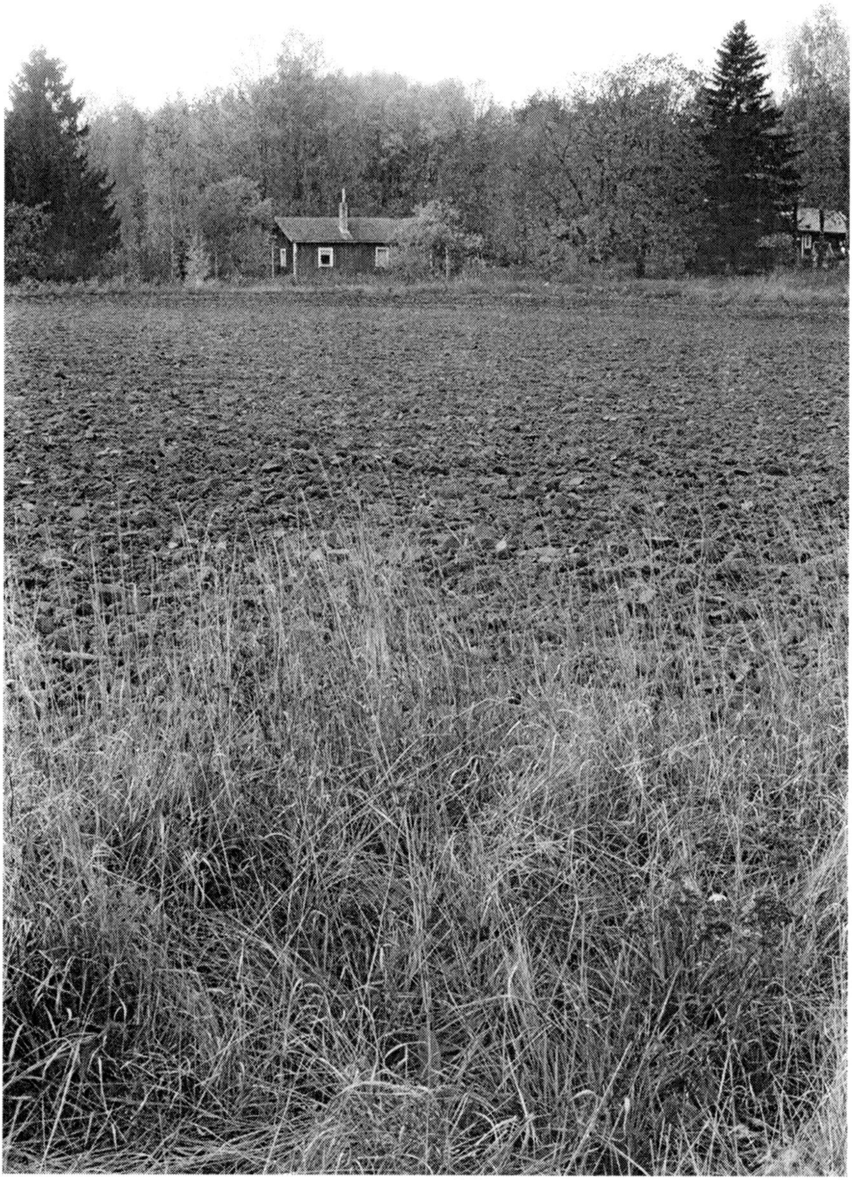

I'm wondering how long it'll take the oakwood to assimilate these stones, for them to weather and leach and to grow into one another in that intricate way minerals and trees have with each other.

It's not Pentti Saarikoski, long dead, but he certainly looks like a photograph I've seen of him with full beard and long flying 1970s hair. He cycles a little past – I think his brakes need attention – then halts and turns his bike and himself round and comes to stand beside me, facing the same direction. He speaks: in Finnish, but when I apologise in English for not understanding the language, he attempts English.

I'm guessing he's about my age. His bike is old, his clothes denim and well worn; world-wide America sits on his head in the shape of a baseball hat. His clear eyes regard me with some curiosity and he makes his thoughts plain in one word and a grand gesture in the direction of where I had been looking: What?

I shrug – how to tell him I'm thinking of the interdependence of mineral and plant? I say one of my three Finnish words: Oak. His eyes wrinkle around the edges Ah! he says, sighing and I warm to a man who can take that as a full explanation.

He speaks again in Finnish and indicates the cloth bag on his handlebars. For a moment I think he might bring out anything: mushrooms, glittering mica, an ammonite, a seahorse.

It's vodka – the cheapest available from Alko, the State monopoly drink shop in town. Leijona brand at 13 euros 25 cents a bottle. I know this because not two hours ago I bought a bottle.

Twisting the screwtop with a crack he offers me the bottle and it's then I say my second Finnish word: Cheers! His blue eyes wrinkle again, he smiles as I swig and hand it back. He swigs and we together contemplate oak. Another swig each and the bottle goes back into the bag.

He's cycled a round trip of 24 kilometres for that bottle. He remounts his bike and points it towards the west again, and my third Finnish word comes out as he cycles off: Thanks!

His smile again and I have no need to understand the words of his reply as he waves his arm up and back. It's a gesture that takes in oak, minerals, age, kitchen chairs, and humanity.

* * *

Life is given to man
to make him consider carefully
the position he'd like to be dead in
Pentti Saarikoski

Tuesday, 14 September 2010
Shiva

Today is yellow where yesterday was green. The butter yellow of the aspen catches my eye. The trees are still vital, but here and there the green is stripped away, revealing the yellow underneath. There is no appreciable difference between the length of light yesterday and today. No difference in temperature that I can feel. Yet all the trees are showing a little yellow; some a lot. Maybe tomorrow the maples will be red.

The aspen leaf between my fingers trembles just as it did on the tree. The aspens, still in full leaf, though yellow, are seething in the wind, each leaf rattling on its stem, making a noise like the gentle soughing of waves onto a strand. The tall birches all droop away from the wind. Maples shed their leaves in their own yellow shadow – falling to windward in a grounded double-image of their upward limbs. Leaves drift down in parabolas to land against the paths, yellow on yellow. The oaks stand against all this, neither much yellowing, swaying nor dropping leaves.

There's a hierarchy of trees which we have imposed. In a woodland there's none of that. I've written before of Shiva (I don't mean the Shiva the god, the destroyer, the bringer of change; though who knows? but Vandana Shiva the Indian physicist and environmental activist) going to the woods to learn of democracy.

What a weasel word democracy has become, though I malign weasels. Self government is what Shiva is really learning from the woods, not a hierarchical trickle down materialism delivered by self-seeking manipulators purporting to represent something they call *the people*.

In a wood, there's balance in the active presence of large numbers of interdependent species; none with greater significance than any other. Aspen leaves and oak leaves alike fall to the forest floor and are pulled down (even in this thin soil) by tribes of earthworms. The woodpecker holes shelter other, smaller birds too. The fungal infestation Ascocalyx abietina has no favourites among the pines it inhabits. Here at Saari, the tree surgeons are in.

Years ago I climbed trees with all the shackles, ropes and harnesses I could muster to give first aid to living broken boughs. It's not a foolproof method of getting up and especially down a tall tree. If you'd ever seen a twelve stone apprentice stuck dangling because of a faulty running knot – and with him two heavy rescuers also stuck for the same reason, and a ground crew in helpless laughter, you'd know the same. But tree surgery has moved on. Here, there's a woman, a man and a cherry picker. And they are pruning the oaks. Only the oaks; of dead limbs.

The value we place on trees, the ranking, that imposed hierarchy, is nearly always financial. The timber will be valuable. So birch is worth less than oak because it's not much use except for firewood; oak is sought after by boat builders and cabinet makers. There's a small island of oaks south of here that was owned by a former Swedish king for building his naval fleets. People, commoners, were kept away from valuable assets (except to cut and haul the trees; ever met a king who did his own work?)

So on the cherry picker basket, thirty feet up, the surgeon is delicately cutting wood with a small chainsaw, as delicate as if with a scalpel. It's not only the oaks that have dead limbs, but the maples too. In a parkland situation like this (built landscape: to resemble savannah with browsing deer where sheep may safely graze for the extremely wealthy) these trees will never be felled for money. They are planting the next controlled and managed generation underneath them; these oaks have become valuable aesthetically (as a former display of wealth, but primarily now for the eye to gaze upon).

It's the aesthetics of the situation that demand the oaks be trimmed, more than the dangers of falling limbs. Maples pose no such threat and are left untrimmed. The tidy civic mind is at work: partial death is unsightly. And let us put the next generation of oaks where it'll be most appealing. Gardening with trees has long been practiced; no different from where the roses go.

The woods, however provide something else. Vandana Shiva may have held philosophical-political conversations with herself in woods. I go to the woods to experience that pleasure of controlled anarchy a woodland brings. Where the fox depends on the mouse, the mouse on the seed, the seed on the pollinating bee and wasp. Where the dead birch leans into the living pine and the bracket fungus slowly reverts to the horizontal as the tree slowly leans in death.

The delight of living, as the other Shiva knew full well, is the awareness of death.

There's no implication of disorder in anarchy; the order of woodlands is neither random nor chaotic, and never destructive. The order of woodlands is self-generative.

I go to the woods because they do not need me.

Thursday, 16 September 2010

Brecht

Ah, what an age it is
When to speak of trees is almost a crime
For it is a kind of silence about injustice!

Brecht wrote that in 1939, while Nazis were burning books and more. Finland was fighting the Winter War with Stalin's Soviet Union and Europe was at war again.

Wars in the twenty-first century are mostly physically removed from Europe, but still often of our making or connivance.

But to speak of trees is not to ignore injustice, and Brecht has that qualifying "almost".

Finland's forested terrain also helped in keeping Finland from Soviet subjugation.

It becomes a necessity to speak of trees more and more as injustices increase. War, even when dressed up in polluting 'ideology' as with the Nazis, is about resources, including land. We are fighting in the middle east for the control of oil and increasingly, of water. That trees and plants, past and present have a role in this is obvious: no laying down in the Carboniferous era of plants, no oil. Without the current stabilising effect of trees, no topsoil, no water retention. When lemon groves and olive orchards are cut down as an act of military aggression in Palestine, it does more than ruin the farmers – it leads to eventual desertification.

To be silent about injustice is not an option. But to speak of trees is not to be silent. It is not only a tacit oppositional stance to that of warmongers, but is also an engagement with some of the underlying causes of war.

Poor people do not own what are now called resources. In Europe, aristocrats once owned vast tracts of forest; some still do. Multinational companies now control the world's resources where once aristocrats did;

the effect is the same, often the owners and controllers are the same too. A discussion of trees is not complete without a discussion of land and land ownership and hence the control of resources.

It's also part of a larger discussion of the way the world is regarded by the ever greedy Homo sapiens (though we should now find a new word to replace sapiens). The most fleeting look at ecology reveals that we depend on other species more than they on us. Our relationship is at best symbiotic, but we act parasitically. The climax of parasitism – say mistletoe in an oak – is the stifling of the host, to the detriment of both.

Brecht was right, we have a duty to act in the prevention of daily – and often terrible – human injustice (there is no other kind). No-one discusses trees to prevent a firing squad or a suicide bomber. But to speak of trees and importantly *for* trees becomes an imperative as well. It's to ask questions; the who, the why.

If a primarily aesthetic (or proper economic) appreciation of trees, of woodlands, leads to an understanding of the political aspects of land ownership and its control and misappropriation; so much the better.

To wander in the woods – where we're not needed – is to realise this. It's also to realise that we're often not wanted by a landowner.

Brecht also wrote: *You can't write poems about trees when the woods are full of policemen.*

Fences are absentee policemen.

Directions

On my flâneur way this morning, I was stopped and asked for directions by two men in a car who wanted to find the water – the sea – and the woods: "the real Finland" as one put it. They spoke in English, I guess having no Finnish, but the irony of asking a man just twelve days in the country for the real Finland amused me. I told them they could not drive there.

I have the sort of face that wherever I go, I'm taken for a local. I've been saluted in Stornoway and hailed in the forest of Fontainebleau; people ask my advice about the destinations of buses. Truth is, I'm just wandering around and frequently lost. Though I feel at home wherever I go, I don't always know how to get from here to there. If I can't read the language of a country I happily rely on the kindness of strangers. Once, in a place where I was effectively illiterate, my direction-giver (a laughter-wrinkled old woman with a roadside stall) took my hand and led me to my destination – a ten minute walk. Deliciously, I was a child again.

Here, since for example I can't understand even the nearby signpost that seems to my ignorant eye to point to Yggdrasil, the world tree, I get by orienting with various landmarks: the clump of old birches, the glade of the mushrooms.

The equinoctial storms are fast stripping not just the leaves from trees, but me of my natural signposts. The old birches no longer look the same; the mushrooms deliquesce in the sudden rains. The geese, an aural marker for me these past days are leaving.

They have circled lazily all my short days here, settling in the bay to my east, muttering into their breasts until night blankets them. With the storms, however, all is activity. I thought them completely flown yesterday, until my ears led me to them in the opposite direction, to the west. Standing in hundreds in a cutover wheat field, up close, their raging discussions in greylag tongue were as loud as they were incomprehensible. Except: I knew instinctively their talk was of migration and the way south. Theirs is a language rich in tonality: the honks and whiffles, the clacks and hoots rising and falling along the scale. The language of the body is easy to understand, though; when they as one spread their wings and made a small run to get airborne, it was clear a decision had been made.

They lifted then, into the wind, the massed lines of their flight-path writing their decision across the grey of the sky in bold quill work: hieroglyphs, ideographs, fine scripts.

Ignorant as I am of even their smallest phonemes, I have enough of their flowing calligraphy to know that it all spells one word: south. Their landmarks remain constant: the waters and the hills; all pointing their direction with the clarity of territory, not the symbols of a map. The oldest lead the youngest: south.

Sunday, 19 September 2010
Entering

What a strange, demented feeling it gives me when I realise I have spent whole days before this inkstone, with nothing better to do, jotting down at random whatever nonsensical thoughts that have entered my head.

So 800 years ago the monk Yoshida Kenko noted in his book *Essays in Idleness*.

Falling short of demented, I nevertheless share Kenko's feelings. While I've been trying for years to *do* less and to *be* more – there's something very odd in the recording of states of being. Or if you like states and places of non-doing.

Although everything else is foraging for a living in the wood, including the trees in the last days of a prolonged summer almost putting on a little extra weight for winter, I'm just sitting here with my back to an old oak.

I'm looking out over flat farmland, due east at the edge of the woods. Here and there an isolated red painted wooden barn settled in a clump of sheltering trees and a big sky above all this flatness.

It's been raining off and on, drizzle mostly, not too wetting, so I'm sitting on my inside-out hat to keep arsebones dry. The great comfort of the woods eases itself into my shoulders. Muscles and bones relax. Behind me are small rustlings and silences. In the silences every now and then I can hear a leaf fall with a papery rustle catching on twigs in its slow descent. The arc of a rainbow appears in the grey sky slightly south of east, its outer edges of red and violet shimmering a little – a result either of the smirr of rain, or my own vision – I can't tell.

I stare so long at the rainbow which shifts only slightly that my eyes dance with entering colour; the woods have folded me in and I drift off into the shortest of dozes, a step beyond reverie.

With solstice right here, right now, earth turning and sun standing, nights already as long as days, this is not idleness. I'm storing up light and colour, a gathering-in of some of the energy of the sun that I'll need to last through the darker days of winter.

Tuesday, 21 September 2010
Autumn folded

> *"When the need for food comes, when you desire to eat,*
> *eat forest mushrooms,…"*
>
> *Charms against bears; the Kalevala*

The day opens with a red squirrel undulating along the road in front of me. I'm off to the woods again still checking mushroom spots as I pass by, and after that to sit awhile in the bird hide, Vasikkahaan. As this is a wetland reserve, as everywhere, the needs of humans are the first to be taken into account, by making a building; though the hide – a tower really to reach above the reedbeds – has me admiring its solid no-nonsense construction.

The bone-headed yaffles – green woodpeckers – seem intent on bashing their brains out on not just the trees, but on the telephone poles leading to the couple of houses at the bay. They pay no attention to me. Like any of the bird-hide's visitors, I hope to see the altogether more shy black woodpecker which is also common here.

A jay scolds me as I pass under her: autumn's folded in her wings and she wants no intruders now.

What the woods reclaim the seasons reveal. I've walked extensively through these woods now for 20 days. How could I have failed to notice the skeleton of a small shed in the centre, collapsed on itself and being absorbed by mosses and lichens, sagging low, so that only the leaf fall of the covering maple is slowly lifting the woodland curtain on this wee puzzling view.

There's none of that damp moss and musty scent in the air that alerts to the presence of ceps. Though there's more fly agaric than I've ever seen anywhere, spilling over themselves at the feet of the old birches: the largest the size of dinner plates and together with the smaller, making up a whole set, side plates, inverted teacups and saucers as well; ranging in colour from deep red to faded yellow that ceramicists would enjoy. But they are not edible. I'm wary of the word poisonous. So often it simply means that the old lore of how to use them has been lost. These were once ingested in animistic belief in these parts. While they do poison – extreme vomiting and diarrhoea – they are seldom killers and (so it's said) grant visions of the seat of illness in a sick person and the location of lost cattle, lost people. There's more to it of course; I simply admire them. The world is odd enough for me anyway without a need any longer to induce hallucinations.

Reaching, eventually, the bird tower, even though I'm pretty quiet in the woods, I disturb a napping buzzard who has time to cast me a look before silently moving off along the wood's edge. I can't restrain myself from laughing at a bird hiding in a bird hide from bird watchers. Though I'm sorry for waking the buzzard.

On my stroll back I'm accompanied by ever increasing numbers of cumulus clouds; east and west and north, wherever I look they're massing, pile on pile. They open the sky: maybe it's the rare glimpses of blue among them. A late cricket hops out of my way on the sandy path.

There's the hot resinous smell of pine in the air and through that the breath of birches. There's flame now in the maples.

Another half crushed viper at the road's edge. I collect the emptied skin of another.

That the fox is there outside my quarters in the old farmhand's cottage is a fine red bracketing, together with the squirrel, of morning and evening in which nothing happens: literally.

Wednesday, 22 September 2010
Sentences from Finland

Acorns crackle underfoot.

Woodstacks grow higher.

Hands clasped behind her back, an old woman in a headscarf watches an old man stooping, lifting some potatoes from the row.

Hidden under his mattress a bar of gold and a revolver.

Thursday, 23 September 2010
Meandering

Following your nose is a fairly common phrase – if not thought about a lot. I'm not sure if it is the foremost part of my body, but I guess I follow it more than most.

It's good to walk into unknown parts of woodland, checking out which jays are feeding off which oak's acorns in their strange jubilant frenzy, not even bothering to scold me. The red of autumn creeps upward in these places with no path; seedling rowans flaming on the floor, maple saplings glowing like any late night peat fire. Oaks overhead still green.

Here's a fine birch – a downy birch, much given to those adventitious clumps of twisted warty growths in its branches – recurving its way up to light – bent at a steep angle by some unknown force before returning to the upright trunk our eyes demand of a forest tree. There's broken charcoal burners (the mushroom of that name) along this way; I'm following the path of deer who'll not bother nibbling the brittle dryness of these – nor will I.

I can hear the geese in the bay – I think (perhaps deluding myself) that I can tell from their gabble that they are Canada geese, not the few greylags left. A woodpecker taps an oak in the afternoon filtered light. I wander on, but alerted by something I can't pin down to move a little to my right. I have no idea where I am in the woods; lost again, my usual state. The canopy is high and blocking any glimpse I might have of the sun. There's no shadows so I can't even tell whether I'm going north or east.

But, and here's the point: here's a wee clearing. On an old stump I smell, then see: chicken of the woods. Laetiporus sulphureus, a strong smelling, sulphur-coloured polypore that puts many folk – mushroom folk, I mean – off. It is of course just delicious. The smell is purest autumn woods and lingers on the fingers and the carefully wielded knife I use to gently slice it from the stump. No druid was ever more careful with an (almost certainly apocryphal) golden sickle. It goes into the yellow cloth bag that travels in my back pocket for just such an occasion.

With a bouncing step, and with the notion that I'm now travelling (no longer following my nose) east; I walk straight to the wood's edge and find the dirt road home. Occasionally I stop and put my nose to the bag, like an eager glue-sniffing lad.

Fried in butter, with garlic, lemon flavoured; both supper and breakfast assured.

Screwcap Letter

Nevertheless, his soul is about to slip through their fingers. As his life ebbs away he wavers, appalled by the thought of an eternity without alcohol, and calls for aquavit.
  Peter Høeg: *The History of Danish Dreams*

Pentti Saarikoski passes this way every day at about 4pm. His beard grows ever longer. He's muttering his latest poem: *we adore other gods here now your feathers are on special offer in the supermarkets.* Today I'm outside, hanging the washing with good wooden clothes pegs on the green plastic line under the Scots pines.

I wave as Pentti cycles past and he wobbles on the bike, slows a little, but continues. I yell and run up the cottage steps and fetch the bottle of Finnish vodka – Leijona Original Viina Brännvin, new, pristine, unopened, the last bottle having sort of disappeared – and hand at the neck of the bottle, wave it, shouting Hey hey!

But he's out of earshot, slipped by, cycling down the hill into what a thousand years ago was the Baltic sea. I'm islanded; but I save that cracking of the vodka bottle screwcap for when he passes tomorrow.

Monday, 27 September 2010
Low moon

> *I seek for charms that autumn best can yield*
> *In mellowing wood & time bleaching field*
>   *John Clare*

The sky is purpling as the light fades. There's a snell wind, but the days are still full of sunlight – dawn to dusk.

It's that sunlight that these trees have been storing, summer following spring, year on year, decades at a time. From the size I'd say fifty years of stored energy giving bursts to growth of limb and leaf, holding back some for those bitter winters that are written through their trunks in concentric circles.

Just now, birch and pine, they're felled, split and stacked in the sauna woodshed. Twelve feet long of a stack, six feet up and six feet across.

There's a melancholy in the air today. Folk are silent, a little withdrawn. There's sunlight in plenty, but there's also that wind, blowing from the east and hopping straight over autumn to speak of winter.

I've missed the sauna time and it's late but I mooch, dragging my toes over there anyway, and at midnight find it still hot. I have it all to myself. There's a greeting from the pine logs and the birch logs throwing their lives of digested sunlight outwards from the stove. I sit on the pine bench and breathe. Simply breathe. My gratitude is to the split logs and Simo the log splitter and to the trees that gave up their stores of energy for this moment.

The axe sits behind the splitting block just outside where I'm suspiring now, rather than breathing. It's a fine tool, with a curve to it that brings to mind those axes carved onto Pictish stones in Scotland; a collar grips the shaft which curves as gracefully as a young birch.

I throw a ladle of water onto the hot stones and a wave of scorched air, seconds in coming, hits the throat and nose first making breathing a searing awareness. I taste the salt of my own lips and at the same time the resinous smell of pine burning is brought to my nostrils straight after the heat.

I'd twisted a calf muscle, but it's uncramping; even my hard-working liver, often a weight on me, seems to relax.

The heat becomes too much, but on my way out I throw on a couple more splits of pine which crackle into flame at once. I cool off in the open porch. I'll not use the dipping pond: it's rank green with duckweed. Just steam in the midnight black.

Distant planets are caught up in the branches of the pines. There's a lowing from the cattle in the one cleared field among the trees down by the bay.

I steam-roast and cool off a few more times, the time in the heat shorter and the cooling longer, until finally the high moon beckons. A dark shadow, stepping delicately through crisp undergrowth, slips among the larch trees over by. The pine and spruce cones are hard underfoot, but the grass is cool and sweeping heels and toes as I walk towel-wrapped, barefoot home.

The living trees softly rolling in the wind, might with me, be recollecting their dead.

Wednesday, 29 September 2010
Here

My walking today on the way to Tammimäke is through a blue sea-sky continuum along the newly raked gravel paths that remind me of that luxurious austerity of some Japanese gardens; but these are for walking on, not just the eyes. The blue is brilliant and though it's full morning, the sun low. Only the belt of trees, their green, breaks up this shining blue.

Overhead fly Canada geese in dozens, their shadows across the gravel and shadows passing quickly up the lit birches. They fly lower and heavier than greylags, their carolling lighter. Memory of place is strong in us all, even when we're passing through, like the geese and me. My walking today is through the places of revealed dreamscape: the small and intimate map made step by step, reading land. I name the places and they exist for my next walk. The place of adders; the bay of the boat-house; the inlet of the blue wooden boat; the apple tree of wasps. Though here all are wasp-ridden, the insects drunk on fermenting juice; but it's at this tree I was stung – picking windfall apples with wasps inside. Our storytelling moves across the land and is a record.

Winter is the stalker in the woods. It's behind the intoxicated wasps, the chittering squirrels laying up stores and the yodels of Canada geese, but summer will not yet yield: its last movement still to be played. A single cormorant flies into the bay from the expanse of the Baltic sea. Jays work the acorns before they tumble to the woodland floor.

This place is called Saari – the Finnish word for island. As well as saari, there are place-names for skerries, rocks, points and sounds all now inland along the Gulf of Bothnia. Oulunsalo (island of Oulujoki) is a peninsula. Turning north and facing the maples on the rise I see quite clearly where the island would have been a thousand years ago, before post-glacial rebound forced the sea to walk from here. I'm strolling on old seabed. Fertile farmland supporting many head of cattle and growing silage and sugar beet.

That long view, were we able to take it, would be the proving of the fact that these oak trees of Tammimäki also walk. Generation on generation, moving out from the parent tree; that oldster dying, leaving this new generation to march outward, until checked, when the trees move back inwards, rippling the years, walking always: slowly walking. A walk of centuries in one place.

On my own day-long flickering ephemeral walk I fill a pocket with rosehips like nipples; I fill my red-spotted handkerchief with puffballs; I carry some stems of yarrow and their pure white flowerheads. These things flame into life and burn out in their walk of shorter days than mine.

The rose hips are for their redness, the puffballs for the skillet, the yarrow for a posy in the jamjar on my desk. I invent these things afresh as stories in my walking, in my memory of place.

Saturday, 2 October 2010
Stored

My grandmother taught me thrift. Each quarter pound paper packet of tea from the grocer was emptied into the tin tea caddy, then carefully taken apart so that not one curled leaf could remain undetected in any fold. The paper was later used to light a fire in the hearth. Tea, any crops, are hard come by however wealthy you are, if you know what goes into the sowing and harvesting. And what comes in between.

I put up with the pricks to my fingers when I'm picking the junipers' berries. I don't mind that a wasp stings me if I'm collecting windfall apples; we can share.

Each yard here has an old apple tree – at least one, often more. Down by where the marsh harriers hunt around Kuustonmaa on the flat sea-reclaimed land there's a yard has twenty trees. I counted them. There seems to be as many varieties of apple in that orchard. A small child plays there collecting apples from the ground and piling them. Many are gone from the trees, safely harvested. The wasps are no more, with days shorter and nights colder. Maybe it was the great grand-mother and -father of this wee girl who planted the orchard, tree by tree, waiting patiently for the first crop after seven years of tending – keeping frosts and deer at bay, the dog chasing rabbits from the tenderness of the young growing stems.

The land farmed here for a thousand years; apples a recent enough introduction, with a crop going into preserves, jams, pies. Some dried. Sweetness before sugar became commonplace.

Fructose – a summer's days stored in each sweet apple. The surplus, when enough had been laid in the cold loft to see a family through winter, sold at market. Essential cash income to small farmers.

Such patience and such rewards. I think of my own tiny orchard at Carbeth, just fruiting its first large crop while I'm away, after those twenty-eight seasons of waiting, spring following winter for seven years. Seven apple-lean years. They're standards mostly and will grow to about fifteen feet high with as big a spread, just as those planted here; grafts onto good rootstock.

There's only nine apple trees at Carbeth and that's planting to the utmost of the available space. All the trees have a connection with children, mine or friends', who get the first fruit each season. The patterns of land and kinship grow strong.

I have no title-deed to that Carbeth orchard and never will. If we succeed in buying the land from the landowner in whose family it's been for generations, it'll be in community ownership. I can only go to the earth, the earth can't go with me. The way it should be.

The old man down the road has brought all his apples in. He used old cardboard apple boxes from a supermarket and his wheelbarrow to move the boxes to the apple loft in his big old wooden barn. The barn itself an old log construction possibly made from the logs from his own felled pines. His driveway is of pines with all the lower branches taken off. They grow straight and tall, plenty of space, plenty light. It's likely he won't see them fully mature. But he grows them on.

How can I know in fifty years who will be eating apples from the trees I planted.

Tammimäki has somewhere between fifty and a hundred mature oak trees. Ten times that number growing up with their roots interlocked and part of the land for a thousand years. The farmers here let them grow in the middle of arable crops. Not sentiment, but there's immovable bedrock upthrusts where the trees are islanded. Nevertheless, each knows the oaks are an inseparable part of this land – no financial value any more, but adding, for just one example, their leaves all and every autumn to the soil's fertility.

From walking around and slowly adding trees to my internal mapping I estimate that there might be a couple of hundred apple trees in the immediate vicinity in farm yards.

In Saffa, summer before last, the valley was set on fire by newcomers: about forty acres burnt clear of shrub and seven hundred trees destroyed. Productive trees, providing that essential income to farmers; planted by grandmothers, grandfathers. Fountains of fire as wee children watched. Soldiers stood by and watched as well, preventing the farmers from quenching the flames, telling them that this is declared State Land, though the farmers have ancient deeds proving the land theirs. People are injured trying to reach their fields, other newcomers act as observers and are helping to try to plant new orchards, with the harassment of the military: this is declared State Land.

My apple trees grow in the wet west of Scotland. This is Finland, where apples are gathered in the burnish of October sun. Saffa is in hot dry Palestine where trees are easily burned to ash.

Watching the flames of family trees, just as I watched granny emptying tea, what is stored in the memories of the children of Saffa?

Monday, 4 October 2010
Knowledge of things

The winged seeds of the Norway maples are spiralling down in their hundreds this morning. I stand face upward and they clatter off me on their way to germination below.

An event in the true sense of the word, as is the dazzling scarlet of the chest of a single high flying bird as she wing-zips into a yielding birch top.

And then to encourage a three foot grass snake to quit the road outside the farm-hand's cottage.

And two feet away a small brown-haired caterpillar on its tread across the road in the opposite direction: I help it across the vast expanse of asphalt, but it curls on itself, becomes a miniature tumbleweed and blows off my hand where it had walked and rolls into the dry stems of rosebay willow herb.

Winged seeds like the maples' are known as samara; I do not know the name of the scarlet chested bird. Linnaeus wrote: "Without names, our knowledge of things would perish." But even knowledge cannot blunt the raw edge of pure awe in seeing scarlet across a blue sky or of a ripple of snake muscle across grey road.

Part heard

> *I love the activity of sound*
> *John Cage*

In that 1991 interview, Cage also quoted Kant: "two things that don't have to mean anything – music and laughter".

I'm staying close to the barn and farmhand's cottage today; it's Sunday and I'm baking bread. There's no-one about and clearly to be heard is the sound of a single aspen leaf oscillating in the coming-and-going breeze from the sea. When the wind freshens a little, I stand under the aspens and they tick like a museum full of clocks. Move a little and the onshore wind brings on the sound of seething water in a pan on the stove. Further off all the aspens together make that noise of a burn running sharply downhill, tumbling across boulders then falling a foot or two.

The maples, Norway maples, Acer platanoides, in the same wind have the sound of surf soughing on the strand.

The first Aeolian harps were not only placed in trees' branches, but must have been inspired by the music of trees in wind. The colours of autumn, or rather the dryness of each tree's leaves colour the sound. These maples are pure fire; the aspens range from butter-gold to green; a shade that brings to mind syboes: tender young spring greens, but in autumn.

There's a red maple leaf: silent, come to rest in falling onto the latch of the gently listing nineteenth century four-seater privy.

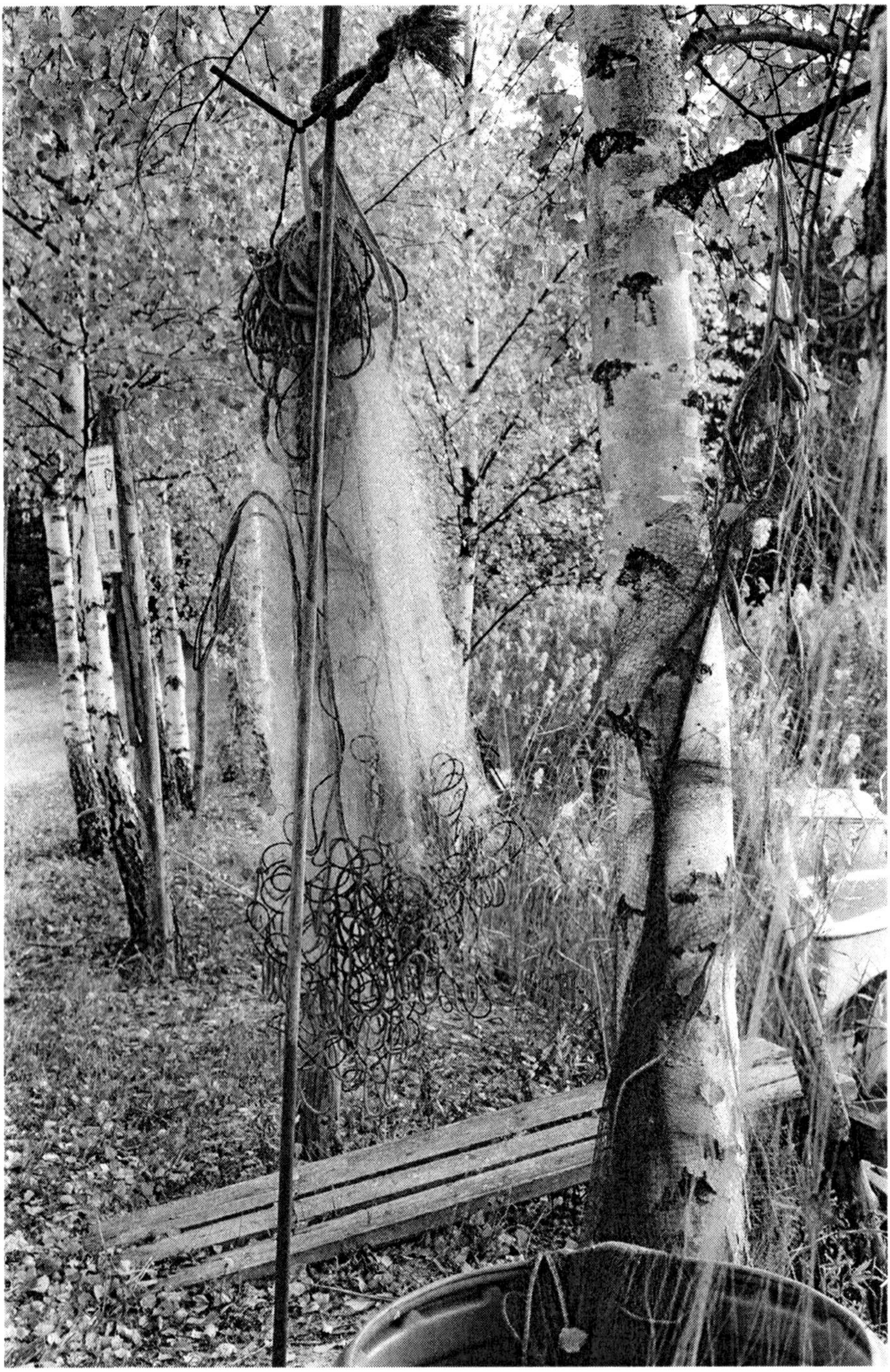

I sit on the sun-warmed stone steps of the granary. It's the highest point of Saari, the former island. I'm somewhere between hearing and listening; in fact I'm not sure here, now, how to differentiate between the two states. One is of attention, perhaps; the other of awareness. There's leaf drop as the oak sheds: one, two three, four: drifting down rustling off branches on the way to the floor.

The counterpoint is the drone and zuzz of fast flying insects. The jay chatter: clicks, whirrs; and shriek. The short trills of fleeter lives than mine. Island music, and always the far-off whooping of Canada geese.

Here's a cricket, sunning like me on the steps to the scribble of my pencil, scratching in the quiet. Dragonflies below the threshold of my hearing, except for a low whirring of the rotor wings of one brown dragon as it settles on my head, who knows in what reverie of its own. The blue-flies' buzz is distant part-heard speech.

The eight sweet notes of a blackbird as rapid as any bat-skreeks and clicks come sudden into the mix.

With ears finely tuned – listening or hearing – could I hear growth and decline, or is that what the hum of the day is?

Could I hear wind whistle through spider webs as it does through a steel wire fence? Could I hear the clicks of communicating wood-ants?

It all happens when there are no expectations. And this music can never be played twice the same.

Friday, 8 October 2010
In the beginning

I've seen the face of God. It's kept in the nearby church at Taivassalo on a Dutch surplice made in 1510 and quite human for a god.

The tree of the crucifix at the altar was made 700 years ago by a great artist. His or her name is lost and the work was hidden for centuries when the Lutheran reformation swung this way.

The Christ, along whose arms wooden blood drips from wounded wooden hands, is angular, elongated yet entirely human in his expression of agony become its own morphic dulling of sense and senses. He is made of lime wood. He is hung on a cross, that oldest emblem of a tree, made from spruce: a beautifully circular paradigm of the living tree become the symbol of itself. The bosses at the ends of the tree's arms are of oak. These woods are practical considerations for a sculptor.

Lime has a stable nature when seasoned and is soft enough to the chisel and gouge, while being robust enough to hold even delicate carving well. Spruce, as any boat-builder would also know, grows straight and true – no curves or knots to this cross. And the oak bosses, never warping, possibly even offcuts from other work the sculptor was making, but perfect for this job. Of course the Trinity is echoed in these three woods.

This whole church might have been made of wood, but instead was made of brick and stone. The brick indicates societal and woodland wealth, albeit in the control of a local aristocrat. It was built in the 1430s and what makes it remarkable, as if the artistry of that cross were not enough, are the glowing brightly coloured frescoes, uncovered in 1890 from two hundred and fifty years of Lutheran whitewash. Protestantism brooks no intermediaries between man and god. There is no need of visual prompts to illustrate creation, so long as there is the bible. In the beginning was the word and the word was with god and the word was god. The absolute primacy of logos over the writhing forms of devils, dragons, martyrdoms, resurrections.

But the sheer vibrancy, vitality of these frescoes, the imagination, the fleshing out of creatures never seen, the faith is something that shakes this cynical old unbeliever: here is beauty.

A pelican feeds her children with her own blood – gushing from her wound – like the Christ dripping limewood blood: it's a dragonish pelican – the painter never having seen such a bird, sitting in a pine tree. The pine is instantly recognisable, though not slavishly realistic and its lower limbs have at some point been pruned – the depiction is accurate of old woodland practices.

St John himself cradles the lamb, but he is dressed in a camel's skin.

Here is the first depiction anywhere in Finland of musicians – one a woman – who plays some percussion instrument now lost to the orchestra; the other – a man – blows baggy-cheeked into a bagpipe.

There is a man-headed creature in a hood, with a dog's body and a fish tail. From his mouth comes not the word, but a curling snaking vine.

In purgatory there are two sinners on all fours with sticks in their mouths, roped face to face at the neck – when one pulls away from the flames, the other burns more fiercely and pulls back; but for eternity: 580 years so far.

The evidence of a deep knowledge of wood types and their management is everywhere to be seen in the work of the fresco painters –

and is as subtle as the work of the artist who made Christ on his wooden tree.

Just behind Saint Peter with his key the size of a small iron gate is a couple of lop-limbed oaks. Their limbs may have been used to frame smaller parts of wooden building: possibly small supporting beams. They may also have been used as fuel for the brick furnaces that would have made such demands on timber that pollarding and coppicing practices will have been widespread. Manage the trees, make the bricks, build the church to house the wooden Christ.

St Christopher carries that same Christ child across an invisible river. Round his calves swim fish that the painter would recognise from this very spot — to this day Baltic herring are caught here and remain a strong part of the economy. Christopher's staff is an entire lopped oak, retaining a topknot of leaves, complete with three remaining roots.

Everywhere, covering walls, arches, corbels is a vast flowering of leaf and green as alive as the medieval woodlands once outside, among which, as today, farmers carve their fields. The church writhes with plant life.

That medieval world effectively came to an end in 1650, when it was painted over and a more sombre colourless world began to be spoken of. *In principio erat verbum.* Except that Latin was banished too. Here, in the medieval church of Taivassalo in the real Finland, with its whitewashed walls and its crucifix banished to an attic, mass was said in the Finnish tongue for the first time ever.

I should relish the word, and I do; but the loss of the timber-and-plant medieval world – that knowledge, existential rather than symbolic (though it worked through its own powerful visual symbolisms) that loss is more than painful. The supremacy of brick, the down rating of wood is the first modernism leading inevitably to our own habitat impoverished times. A straight path to the debased political manipulations of language that the rule of the word, or the Word, if you prefer, made possible.

There can be no intercession between man and the Word. The trees are painted out.

Saturday, 9 October 2010
Väinämöinen's oak

In order to reach the small island community of Iniö, maybe twelve miles from here down the bay and out into the Gulf of Bothnia, if you don't have a boat (and I don't) it's necessary to travel by bus maybe forty five north and then turning south west to negotiate the bays, inlets and islands scattered along the coastline. Then the two ferries, first to the island of Jumo, then another to Iniö.

While I'm here to look at the oakwoods – unusual for Finland, the country of pine and birch, I need to get an idea of the bigger landscape in which they formed. Waterscape would be as correct as landscape with twenty thousand islands in the archipelago.

The road north starts with surprises for me – among the spruce and pine, fir and birch in large tracts, broken only by farmland – crops of sunflowers and of raspberries. After the raised eyebrows, I realise the length of summer days and relative mildness (it's comparative) are responsible. As must surely be the case with the long growing oak.

We move on edging south west into a place full of lakes and rivers, each with tiny mooring places and boathouses, inlets bounded by rock outcrops with the trees in feathery mossed bedrock cracks. Causeways and bridges lead the way, which becomes almost more water than land, more rock than farm, more woodland than all those. In this landscape, in this place it's easy to believe in the presence of not just the bears and wolves still here in forest and told of in the Kalevala, but the legends around them, of Väinämöinen's sowing of the ancient wilderness itself:

He sowed the hills with pine groves, sowed the knolls with stands of fir
He sowed birches in swales, alders on light-soiled lands
rowans in holy places, willows on flooded lands
junipers on barren lands, oaks by the side of a stream.

The names of the places we pass or are signed are the melody of epic: Lautenpää, Rautila, Taivassalo, Pukholma, Lehtinen, Aasmaa, Hakkenpää, Parattula and Laupustentie.

The first ferry is Aurora. The chart on the cabin wall shows me absolutely that there is as much land – island – as water. I find it hard to get a bearing on where we might be, with islands to each horizon, with hard by, tree'd island on isle on islet, skerry on reef; up close, and we are, these are upthrusts of weathered granite with the trees clawing into fissures. And we're floating not only on the water the ferry sails, but on the reflected mass of piled cumulus.

Iniö kirk is a beautiful spare Gustavian building. Indeed it was Gustav IV who had it built in 1798, perhaps fearful of the Revolution in France, building churches for merit in the next kingdom. The white interior is loved by the priest who tells us not only of the strong grace of the kirk architecture, but of the people who live on the island. There's a small community of 250, with two schools, a shop, a post office, a nurse, a library visiting twice a week and a doctor visiting once or twice a week. And the ferry is free.

Inside the doorway of the kirk proper, beyond the entrance leading to the belltower hangs a small model three-masted schooner. In august and spare Gustavian surroundings I find it heartening to find this *ex voto*. With prayer, it brings sailor and fisherman safely home.

I climb, with the priest to the very top of the bell tower – she's a little nervous of the open sided stairway at the very top, but we make it just fine, among a couple of fossil like bird skeletons and a fluttering finch. The finch has come in through a gap in the wooden shutters and disturbs the priest greatly – she'll return later to make sure it's away.

At the top, above the two bells, the vast oak beams are scrawled with the names of the old carpenters and repairers. Some have taken a chisel and carved, most a stub of pencil and written names and dates in copperplate handwriting as fine as the beams themselves. The priest speaks with fondness of the descendants of some of those who have written their names.

The easy-going island ways mean that a mention of the bells demands that the bell ringer be phoned to ring them, though it might mean the islanders wonder who they are tolling for.

And he duly arrives, a farmer in boiler suit and cap, speaking an elegant island Swedish, as though Gustav was still around. The bells – after introductions – are rung. I'm in the tower with ear protection and watch as the bell-ringer muscles the bells into heavy chimes – no ropes, but short cords (looking like baling twine) to each bellhead which is swung to rebound the clapper. One bell, one ring, the other bell, another ring, repeated and repeated. I feel all this as much as hear it. The bells are cradled and swung in massive oak squared beams.

The ferry, the Skagen had brought us to the north settlement here, Norrby, so I head south to the other end's village, Söderby. It's an island of boats, though we pass the mandatory island rusting cars at farmroad end – old Volkswagens, each costing more to move to scrap than it ever cost to buy. It's a living island, full of apple trees and caravans, with those boats at Söderby tucked into fine boathouses and mostly out of the water. A couple of steel working boats pull against the ropes; a classic wooden island two master rides beautifully each small swell in the wee harbour.

A living island anywhere has its problems, too, with folk far away inheriting country cottages here – there's more than half a million in the old wooden-hut tradition of city escape now in Finland; with these driving the price of houses, it's hard for the youngsters to find somewhere to live. The old island troubles and concerns remain of course. The priest tells of the old lore of winds – which not to set out in; which will bring rain. And above all which quarter's wind will bring the fish which mean winter food.

The midsummer tower is still here at Söderby, with four ships at the top spinning in the wind, the rowan leaves twined through it now brown. Soon it will come down until summer rises again in Iniö and the archipelago.

The little oakwood at Saari is inseperable, not just from the land that allowed it to grow – or maybe Väinämöinen had a hand – but from the people and their lives, who still cherish trees and the use of timber in church and boat.

Back on the Skagen and midway between Iniö and Kustavi there is a little transforming magic: the spirit of place, oak and pine and sky and rock takes over, somehow an inversion of island and sky – the skerries, reefs and whitecaps rising into the blue overhead and the same number of small drifting cumulus clouds buoying the Skagen from below.

The ferry drifts this way, between clouds, with tree'd islets above until two shadows arrive moving somewhere between: a pair of white-tailed sea eagles out-skerry size pass languidly, making small the laboured distance of the Skagen's engines.

Louhi, mistress of north farm, takes her broken boat and fashions it again:

> *…the planking she knocked into wings,*
> *the steering oar into a tail for herself…*
> *She spreads her wings to fly, raises herself aloft like an eagle*
> *She flies swiftly along, seeking out Väinämöinen;*
> *one wing brushed the clouds, the other grazed the water*

Thursday, 14 October 2010
Plenty and enough

> *October days ride seven horses*
>   *Finnish saying*

The first snow of the season fell softly this morning, quietly and with no fuss.

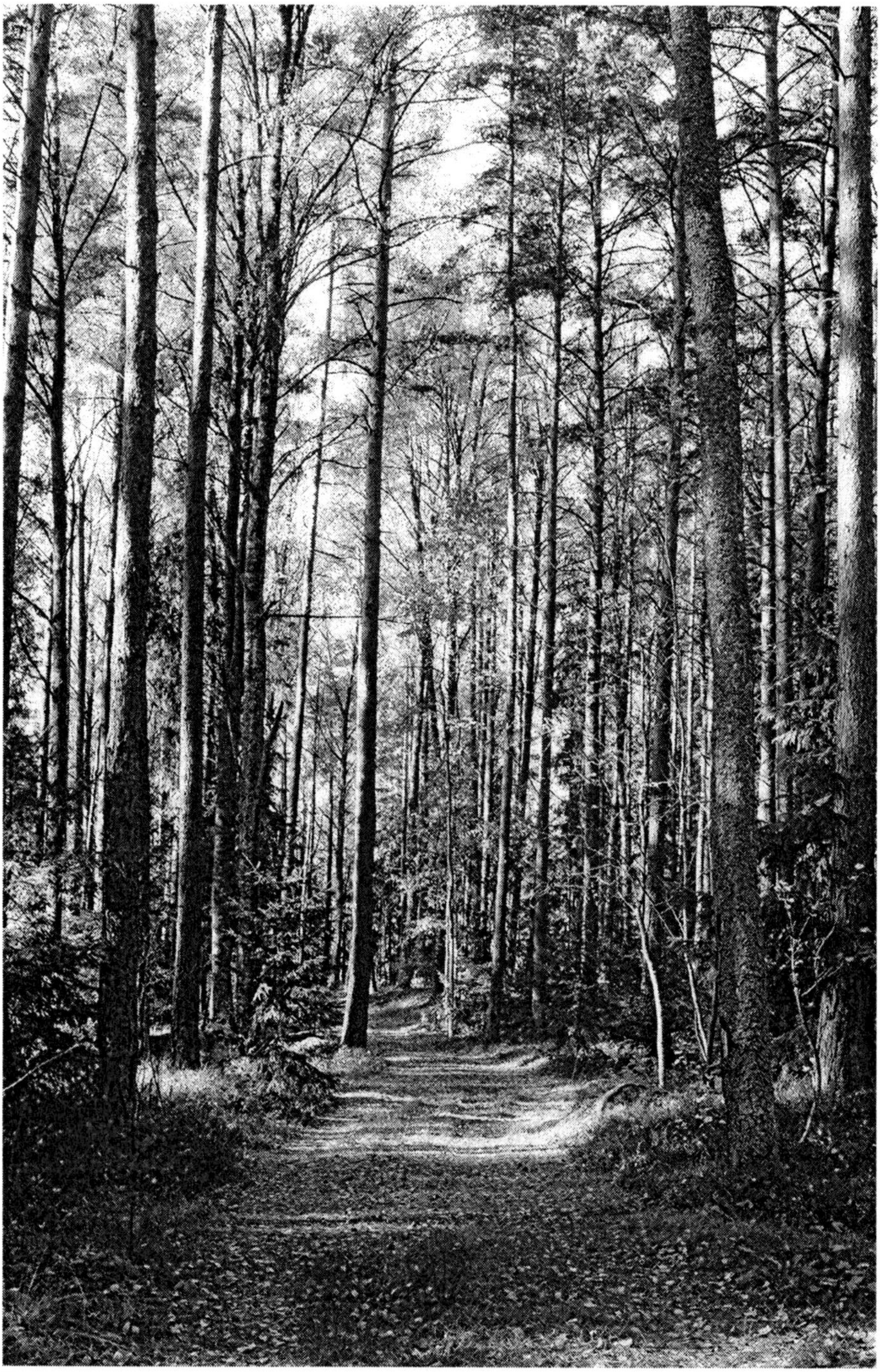

By the time I got to the lower tower with jays squabbling all around me, the tide was out and the tower was swaying slightly in gusts of wind that followed on from the snow. The wind had alternated with hail and dazzling sun.

The top of the tower in the middle of the wetlands is level with the straight-growing pines' and birches' uppermost branches, maybe 36 or 40 feet up. The trees' tops are close enough to reach out to and today in the east wind they lean over right into the open tower.

The jays are constant in their bickering and only a solitary grey crow flies purposefully on her errand against this east wind. A finch hurtles by on a squall followed by a leaf of birch at almost the same speed. Five swans beat up and away, black in silhouette against the sun.

The sun kindles odd corners of the woodland now that the leaves are thinning, sending shafts to search the woodland floor, revealing silent citadels of wood-ants. Bullfinches flicker from floor to low branch seeking shelter; despite the snow and hail and the lip-cracking east wind and eyebright sun; despite cold biting nosebones and seeds hidden in leaf drifts, their fleeting brightness seems to light seeds in front of them and then over there and then elsewhere.

For me too, on low shrubs there's plenty of fraochans and enough lingonberries for my tongue to remember summer.

Snow makes the event; taste liberates the body's memory. Whatever it is that happens, it happens here.

Sunday, 17 October 2010
Time-givers

The barn is made of wood, the cladding of pine planks. It's red painted and glowing in the low evening sun. The shadow, of the big poplar tree, older than the barn, is cast against the gable end and its topmost branches reach to the roof ridge and below that the lower limbs are shadowed in perfect symmetry. The trunk and its shadow are the precise straight perpendicular axis of not just the barn, floor to apex, but this exact cold autumn evening as well. The sun is at a level with both tree bole and gable end; balanced, poised, halted. Everything is caught and folded into the spirit of place.

A provocative harmony is manifested here, as if those zeitgebers – time-givers – of Circadian rhythm have switched attention to a century measure, away from day's cues and have lit up this relationship of elegant distinction, in which the man-made is stamped fleetingly with the poplar's seal of approval.

Monday, 25 October 2010
Heart of the sauna

Nothing: what the mind amounts to.

A relief, then, dripping onto pine boards; pine, pine and birch burning on the stove, pine planking inside straight pine logs, adzed and trimmed a hundred years ago and laid true.

Wood, fire, water. Water thrown on hot stone to steam and become instant dry steam heat alchemy: nothing; no thought other than of wood and become elemental. With steamheat, with eyelids calmed, heart slowed, mouth heat-cleansed. No-mind no-thing.

And back to the cottage, barefoot through sleet and ice-stiff grass.

Lambency

The last bus drops me off at the road end in full moon: a hunter's moon. The air is crisp and clear; the temperature very low.

Snow poles are out all along the roadside, though there's no need of them tonight.

The sky is clear too; nothing but the moon and a few stars: the Plough, Venus. It's not hard to imagine the blue light to the north is the aurora borealis, what's called here fox fire. The story goes that an arctic fox was running in the far north, brushing his fur on the mountains as he passed, causing sparks to fly up into the sky, becoming the northern lights.

Foxfire is also the bioluminescence of some species of fungi that enjoy decaying wood, like the Armillaria species: honey mushrooms – also good to eat, but I've seen none here along by the woodland.

Aside from the moon, there's a small fire of brushwood and brash left over from recent fellings way out in a pale newly ploughed field. The moon illuminates its smoke.

Moonlight lifts the long white plastic bale lines of silage waiting to be brought home so that they appear floating, luminous above their shadows. My shadow walks companionably beside me, merging with the shadows of roadside trees, but always emerging again and stepping to my steps.

Shadows are fewer where the trees are thin; the moon strikes right to the woodland floor in pale shafts, dappling the fresh frosted leaves, sparking a hundred lights. A fallen aurora.

Just before the dark woodland – pine and oak and birch, alder and spruce – a slender shadow of a tall thin birch is cast all along the whole lit length of an old oak-bole's crinkled skin. That too merges with my own shadow as I pass.

It's so seldom that I walk at night, I'd like to prolong this short walk – half an hour is not long enough; and though there's plenty of white on the white page to write these words, zero degrees mean it's too cold to linger.

I breathe a last plume at the night sky; my shadow does the same, then I move inside the old farmhand's cottage; but I move around inside by moonlight, stepping where moon fingers the wooden floors.

Light's not just what strikes into the eye. It's what a fox delivers, a mushroom on dying wood; it's ciphered in the whorl and mottled grain of wide old oak floorplanks. Shadow is nothing but the far side of what we see.

Posterity

Tikka päätään puulun nakkaa

muttei loukkaa
koskei lakkaa
    (Lauri Viita)

I'm out of the woodland for a while, visiting Tampere, but the woodland isn't out of me.

Tampere is an interesting place. Here, two lakes almost meet, one fifty-nine feet lower than the other: Näsijärvi and Pyhäjärvi, only the town, squat on its landmass keeping them apart.

That fifty-nine feet led the Glaswegian James Finlayson, a Quaker Victorian capitalist, to build a cotton mill here in 1823 – the mill race and enormous factory bearing his name in stone are still here. Finlayson is the man credited with bringing the Industrial Revolution to Finland – a dubious distinction.

Tampere's also the place where Stalin first met Lenin at the Bolshevik Party Conference of 1906. During the Finnish Civil War Tampere was a Red Guard stronghold; the last Reds were killed in 1918 at the highest spot of what was then a small village outside Tampere: Pispala.

Pispala was built to house working men and their families, high on the moraine ridge between those two lakes. I'm here as guest of the Scottish poet Donald Adamson, who lives at Pispala. Which brings me back to the woodlands.

Donald's house is next to the house of Lauri Viita, the carpenter; a son of a carpenter, and a poet steeped in that socialist and working class tradition that seems to pervade Tampere and Pispala still.

I can't help wondering about the wood Viita used in his daily trade; what timbers his father built houses from. I know that they will have used both pine and oak. Oak, being scarce and locally confined in Finland, likely will have come from around here at Tammimäki or perhaps even from Ruotsalainen, the island once owned by the king and which was his oak preserve for war-fleets. I like that circle of a working man reaping the benefits of a monarch's belligerent paranoia.

Later, after fighting in the Winter War and the Continuation War, Viita wrote his first book, never losing sight of his political allegiances:

Some voice is explaining:
– This is that sick head
in which the lunacy is bread.
Is it a leak in the mould, a blast
in the alloy, or a fault in the cast?

At the end of his life he wrote sometimes in the Kalevala metre; maybe something of those oak beams and Väinämöinen at his heart.

There's a museum to Viita in Tampere; the building in which it's housed was built in part by his father.

There's a museum to Lenin, too; I don't know who built that.

Finlayson built his own museum – a cotton mill – and had his name carved on it.

The Viita part-poem I started with: *Tikka päätään puulun nakkaa*, I love the sound of. It roughly translates (I'm told) as: the woodpecker bangs his head, but never hurts it.

This morning early, down in the oak wood, I saw a green woodpecker, sitting as though she'd had enough banging for one day already. While there's no official museum for the woodpecker, the tikka, this whole oakwood serves that purpose. Lauri Viita, poet and carpenter, would understand.

Wednesday, 27 October 2010
Diamond

Ten feet from my window – I've paced it – there's a deep steep-sided ditch. It's a channel for water, of course, but also a highway for small rodents. Seconds ago a buzzard stooped, fast, into the ditch. I could see her brown mottled feathers, her spread wings among the dead, still-standing grasses that line the ditch. Jays screeching like the demented inmates of some former bedlam. I'm thinking the buzzard has stooped on one of them, when she jumps, takes off with a gallus wingbeat. In her claws a long tailed field mouse.

Yesterday a large raven, high overhead the cottage was boldly flyting a sea eagle, making that deep musical chiming call. Above, then below: the raven was doing his best aerobatics, but never coming too close to the claws of the sea eagle.

The raven has a wingspan of about four feet. The sea eagle's eight foot span dwarfed the bold raven.

The sea eagle coasted on, higher, then higher still, ignoring the raven. As the buzzard had been apparently oblivious to the squawking jays.

Raptors have diamond pointed minds.

Suppilovahvero

Everyone's hungry this morning.

I'm out early looking for late chanterelles – the tubiform kind with black tops and yellow stems. They have no English common name; I call them yellow-legs, the Finns call them suppilovahvero. Cantharellus tubaeformis. It's been wet lately and not too cold – good conditions and the right time and place: the woods.

Overnight, though, everything has turned to silver. Frost reaches right up into the trees. Frosted spider webs cross the paths. There are frozen deer slots at the wood edge, hard set and clear.

A red squirrel, actually a ruddy brown, stirs herself from a reverie of cold as I walk by; acorns are frozen to the ground where they fell. We regard each other solemnly, as folk who realise that autumn is over. The last aspen leaves are tumbling too, early sun touching the tops of the trees and releasing the stems from the grip of frost.

My old friend, the fox, kettu, hears me coming crackling leaves underfoot and makes his near invisible, silent russet way off along the path through falling buttery aspen leaves and frosted brown oak leaves.

Jays are beginning to flash about, pinkish and part blue-winged, singing a little. They sound the way squirrels should sound. But more are noticing me and scolding from one side, then echoed on the other.

The cold makes us all cranky. I've little hope of finding yellow-legs among all these falling yellow leaves, so being pragmatic will head back and have a breakfast egg without mushrooms. I have the choice; fox, jay and the others must forage all the harder.

And it'll get harder too. As I get back to Saari, Simo is using an old drill to make holes for snow poles in the frozen ground next the driveways. They look a little gay, a little odd – they are made from the tops of spruce trees with topmost branches still intact, needled thickly. Snow is on its way.

Thursday, 28 October 2010
Presence

There are still things in the world that cannot be bought or bartered. Some things cannot be worshipped or derided, not even touched or held; yet here, now, worldly; tenacious, solid flesh and muscle and brain.

This morning passing through the air in and above my soil-born world, the impossible grace in passing of seven impossibly slender and muscular El Greco elongated common cranes.

They are silent. I'm jubilant; almost making their bugling noises in my own throat as I salute their fleeting presence; our joint existence in this very world.

Carpenters' work

> *Bear, apple of the forest, honey-paws with arched back...*
> *Golden cuckoo of the forest, lovely shaggy-haired one...*
>
> *Väinämöinen addresses the Bear, The Kalevala*

What are the consequences and materiality of a culture and tradition of wood use? The filigree and decoration as well as the practical construction and materials and tools?

I don't really expect to see the bear in the forest, but it seems worth a trip to Karelia in the east, the entire width of the country away. Where city road signs read St. Petersburg; not quite in Russia, but in Finnish Karelia: the rest of Karelia was ceded to the then USSR after the 1939-40 Winter War that raged here, with Finland a small republic torn between large militaristic neighbouring dictatorships.

Väinämöinen was not known as a particularly peaceful man, starting fights with everyone he met, including epic battles with the Mistress of North Farm.

My first sights on walking by Lake Saimaa into town are of tanks: one German-, one Russian-made, both bought in the last century's war for the Finnish Army. The reality of crude machine brutalism designed to kill and maim is always a surprise.

The Swedish name of Lappeenranta, Vilmanstrand, translates as Wild Man's Shore, though might not refer to Väinämöinen or the Apple of the Forest.

The Kalevala stories were collected largely in Karelia by Elias Lönnrot. That music, poetry and song, playing itself to me is reason enough to visit Lappeenranta in Finnish Karelia.

Linnoitus, the fortress on the hill overlooking the harbour is another surprise. Through three hundred years, passing through the hands of Swedes, Russians and Finns in wars with names like The Great Wrath and used as a prison during the 20th century, today the elegant barracks have been converted to warm comfortable modern museums: South Karelia Art Museum, South Karelia Museum. Here is the oldest Orthodox church in Finland, smack opposite the Cavalry Museum.

It's cold here and I've been walking all morning. The fortress has also a cafe; though that is to underestimate the effect it has on a cold man entering. In a room full of antique sofas and tables is the largest selection on a side buffet table of berry pies, chocolate cakes and Karelian pies possible; in the largest possible helpings. A bear would sit and quietly eat through it with me; these cakes are probably the closest I'll get to honey-paws.

But it's at Linnoitus, a strange place for delicacy, that finely preserved wooden buildings display that materiality of culture I'm in search of. The construction and decoration of the buildings demonstrates a deep knowledge of and love for wood. The diagonal quartered door panels – when they could be plainly horizontal or perpendicular – show not only an eye for the way wood grows, but make use of shorter planks than other styles of door panelling. The filigreed planking at wall tops also protects beam ends. The low, wind-resistant solid length of the architecture itself reflects huge fallen trees.

It's not fanciful to find faint traces of the songs of Kalevala in carpenters' work. Songs, people and buildings grew alongside and within Finnish forests – here Karelian – where old honey-paws walks to this day. Through yesterday's wars and the consumerism that sits below in the town, here is a continuity, a culture still cherished, but above all lived through and in.

Väinämöinen sang to a birch tree before cutting it for a new harp:

Do not weep green tree!
Do not keep crying, leafy sapling! Do not lament, white girdled one!
You will get abundant good fortune, get a pleasanter new life.

and then after cutting:

There is the body of the harp, the frame of the eternal source of joy.

Väinämöinen is referring to the music the harp brings; but also to the joy of the labour of carpentry, of the skill of working and love of wood, of the knowledge of trees and the forest and its dwellers.

I know carpenters who select wood with equal care and who are aware that they work part of a once living organism taken from a living woodland. It's the old way. Found here in Lappeenranta.

With only one daylight short visit here the big lake beckons. Lake Saimaa is difficult to walk round, even though I start by walking down Lönnrotinkatu – Lönnrot Street. I catch a bus for Saimaa Canal, the waterway between Saimaa and Vyborg, now part of Russia, always Karelia.

Woodland shores of the lake are encroached by urban life; a long motorway bridge arcing high leads to Taipalsaari, one of the largest islands. But here, walking along by water is old Karelia still: an old wooden barn, with wooden scaffolding up the southern side. It's being re-thatched. The farmhouse stands nearby as does the sauna. For all I know it's called North Farm.

I shamble to my night's rest the other side of Lappeenranta, by the shore of Saimaa, in the dusk, cold, hungry and content. I knew I wouldn't find the bear, but I found his dwelling place; and somehow, "the splendid fellow himself" found me.

Friday, 29 October 2010
Establishment

> *Down the ages*
> *they conduct their long monologue:*
> *can't you hear?*
>
> Mirkka Rekola

I'm struggling towards a notion of experiment here.

Saari is no backwater, though it's rural. In 1761 Augustin Ehrensvärd moved into Saari Manor. A soldier, a count and an architect, he had a deep interest in the arts and natural sciences, perhaps like me seeing not much difference between the two. He was a good friend of the great Swedish naturalist Carl von Linné – Linnaeus, and some time in that decade wrote to Linnaeus asking his advice on agricultural experiment at Saari:

"I have … a plot of 24 tunnlands that is under salt water each spring, and would thus seem suited to the purpose. The earth is sandy. … I have thought [of] experimenting with growing rice."

At the same time, perhaps known to Ehrensvärd, in New England settlers had also been trying this, though with what success can be imagined. Linnaeus was enthusiastic, but there are no rice-paddies ever recorded at Saari (nor New England as far as I can tell). Short summers and dark frozen winters may not help, however sandy your soil.

In 1959 Agrifood Research Finland took over Saari Manor and made cropping experiments and research here on clay land, including seed testing. They only left five years ago. Many of the apple trees the scientists planted still bear fruit and are delicious; though some others mysteriously wither on the bough or are dry when bitten.

A thousand years ago Saari was an actual island, surrounded by a small flotilla of others – the archipelago reaching right in here. One such small island was Tammimäki. It's now impossible to determine whether there were oaks at that place back then, but when the water receded, if not there already, the seeds came.

It's possible, though, to see the great waves of land-history, with glaciers retreating, sea levels falling and flora and fauna moving in to take the place of water and ice as linked to the later experiments of Agrifood scientists and Ehrensvärd. Sand deposits, boulder-clay soils a gift to agriculturists of every period.

Oakwoods are rare elsewhere in Finland; round here are plenty: placenames tell that story – always on higher ground – all islands once. The first experiments are always those of the land: best land use determined by climate, seed availability, soil type, geology and altitude; achieving perfect self-management without human intervention. Balance, and at the same time, constant flux; and working with that to achieve a harmony of mineral and soil, flora and fauna, that I can only incline my head to.

The oakwood of Tammimäki is a manifestation of successful earth experiment. We may walk under the oaks, but we are not needed. Terrain established and thriving.

Growth

Is there room on the island, land on the main part of the island
for me to sing my songs, intone my long lays?
Words melt in my mouth, sprout on my gums.
...

Then reckless Lemminkäinen now began to sing.
He sang up rowans in farmyards, oaks in the middle of farmyards,
sturdy boughs on the oaks, an acorn on a branch.
        The Kalevala

Ruotsalainen is an island of oaks.

Not a big island, like nearby Ruissalo, which has a larger oakwood, but with ancient oaks, mostly overlooked by timber hunters. They were owned by the King of Sweden. The people of the island once came to hate the oaks as symbols of an unloved monarchy. The oaks are still there; the king long gone and his wooden fleets (for which the oaks were preserved) with him.

Sadly, although well served by their government, few islanders are left in the twenty-first century. The Turku archipelago and its sometimes difficult winter climate has shared a rural decline with much of the rest of Finland.

My hosts at Saari have arranged a special trip for me to see the oaks. There's a regular ferry for the islanders, but there's no facilities on the island for anyone else. Twenty-one folk live here.

The ferry-crossing is bitterly cold this October day; all my layers are cut right through by the wind. Sisko Ilmalahti, our guide for the day (our wee group is Anna from Saari, Morven, Niran, myself and Alpo the dog), greets us at the ferry landing and accompanies us directly to her house for coffee and an early lunch. Islanders eat early and heartily. Her house is off by a small bay, surrounded by piles of anchors.

The heavy horse left the island two days before we arrived, but evidence of its work is everywhere. They've felled some trees in the woods: not oaks – pines mostly, and big ones at that. Any fool can fell a tree. What happens then is a large tractor entering the woodland, compacting earth, destroying flora, including saplings, breaking overhead branches, to drag or worse, load out the stems on a heavy trailer.

The best woodland management is the oldest. Here, they've felled the trees not for the timber, though of course, nothing will be unused from trunks to lesser branches, but for the light their absence brings to the woodland. The horse has trodden carefully round all saplings, its heavy weight nothing compared to the tons of a forestry tractor. Its chains and harness, its strength and intelligence alongside its handler's mean each tree is hauled out, slowly and with care, bringing trunk after trunk with no more damage than the walk through the woods we're taking now.

Oak trees seem now to need a great deal of light if they are to grow from acorns which fall from trees onto the woodland floor. Regeneration needs a little help. Sometime around 1900 there was the accidental introduction into Europe of American oak mildew, which spread to every deciduous oak in Europe. While not deadly in itself, its effect is to add to the burden of oak saplings attempting to grow under a heavy canopy; the combination of mildew and absence of light does mean death to the saplings, however. Acorns carried by jays or squirrels outside the

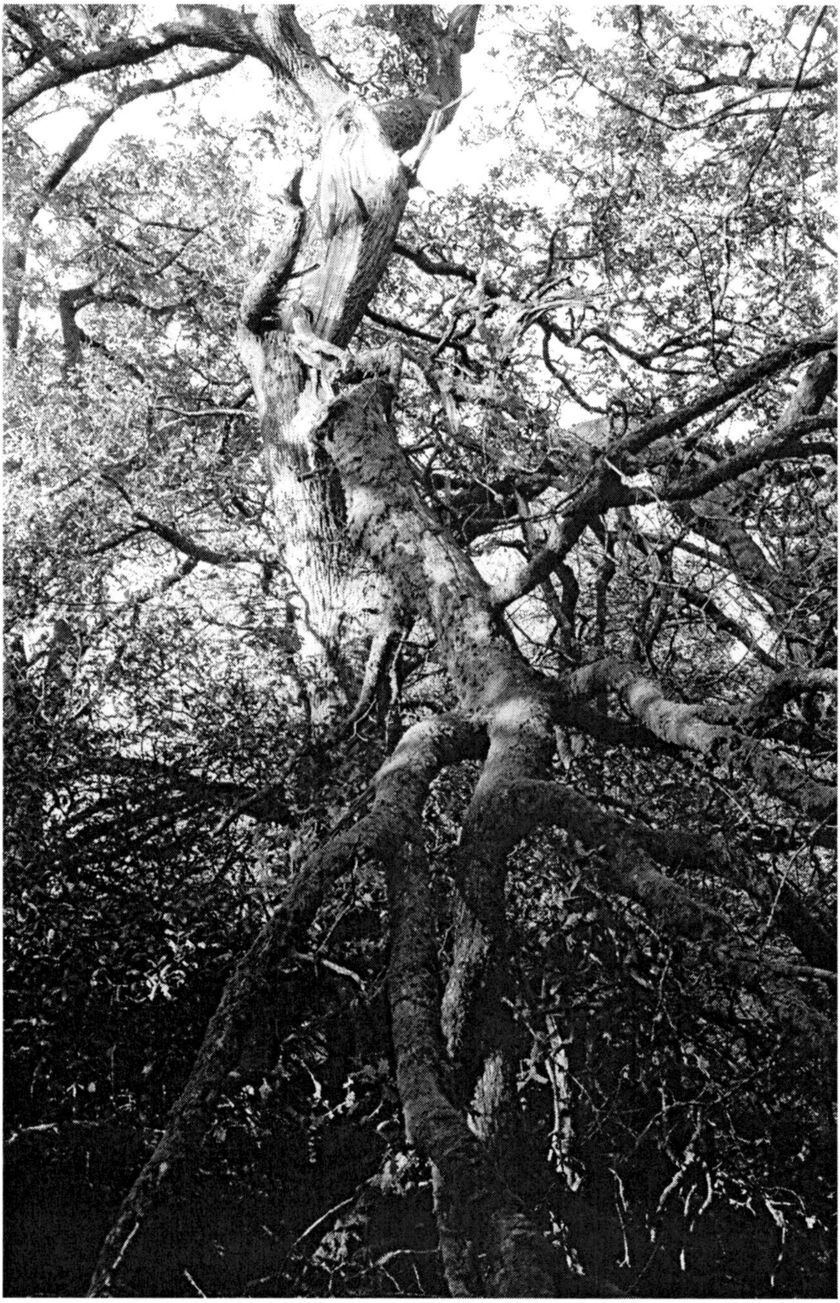

woodland, buried and forgotten grow perfectly well. Oaklings now grow happily anywhere except in oakwoods.

Here on Ruotsalainen, they want to rejuvenate this precious woodland – there's nowhere for acorns to germinate on an island except inward to the oakwood – hence the felling for light and the great care taken by that horse avoiding oak roots and already struggling oak saplings.

There's snow flurries, with fat flakes landing on the floor as I stand at the foot of an ancient, broken-limbed oak with Sisko's husband. Morven's stravaigin somewhere, doing her thing with the old slide camera and Anna has wandered off with Sisko looking for mushrooms. There can be no better companions to a forest than the quiet hunters of mushrooms and photographs and this island-forester weighing each word with myself and Niran, an environmental artist, who's thoughtfully translating.

We estimate the tree to be older than five hundred, but there's no way of knowing for sure without a core sample, which would be foolish with such a precious tree. We talk of ancient island grazing regimes; of how islands are washed over not just by heavy seas, but by history. Forgotten woodlands the man's saying, which allowed them to survive.

We talk a long time, round the tree, looking up, with snow falling on our faces, knowing that all is being done to help the woods live on into a time we'll never see. We stroll across a small clearing to another oak oldster and continue the discussion at its foot. I do my nose to outstretched arm's fingertip circling – an infallible yard-length each time – and the old tree gives me five and a half yards of circumference. The conversation is perfect and slow as growth; but Anna calls across the woods asking if we're waiting for winter. And we realise we're cold and hungry. Anna has found fat perfect ceps and shows us her haul as we struggle back the long way to the anchored yard.

On the way, we pass the manor house and its outbuildings – wood of course, with a windvane carrying the date 1677. The timber ends of old log-built barns have been used to help date woodlands elsewhere in Finland, but these are too weathered. The date though and the size of the great foundation timbers, old when felled, points to an ancient woodland of oak on the island in the middle ages – the time of Taivassalo kirk with its peopled and demoned landscape frescoes.

The islanders have ever lived in the present though and have tried everything to put food on the table. We pass a low deserted part-brick building with a date of 1928: there was a brief attempt then to establish a brick manufactory with local clays, but it never amounted to anything in Depression times; islanders staying with the fishing and farming.

Along the way too, we clamber up the weathered outcrop at the centre of the island. It's no longer snowing, the skies are blue and we're treated to a 360-degree view of small islands, skerries and trees wherever they can crimp their roots. To each horizon: islands and trees.

Back at her house, Sisko busies herself with cooking another meal on her old steel log-range; Anna cooks up the mushrooms and we talk with Sisko and her husband about island life. The TV is on in the corner, sound down: an incongruous documentary about logging truck drivers in Alaska. In gaps in the slow moving conversation, we all stare out the windows – each one with a different view of up-close pines and birches, with flittering tits; between the trunks the glimmer of cold Baltic water. A helicopter can be heard away to the south, then seen: it's the mainland hospital helicopter. Sisko tells us they don't turn out if the patient is very old. I don't know if this is twenty-first century health economics or that the helicopter ride would prove too much for a frail old person.

Sisko was born on Rekisaari, King's island, which she says should be pronounced Reksaari. It's called that because the king (him of the oaks) visited once. Her great-great-grandfather was a Pilot in these waters which are deep, mostly narrow and very difficult unless one knows the reefs and rips. Her great-grandfather and his son were Pilots too. Children are baptised here in sea water – that way they'll not drown at sea.

Sisko and her husband came to Ruotsalainen to build this house as a summer house sixteen years ago. No-one now lives on Rekisaari. Sisko shows us a photograph of herself and her father and brothers all smiling from 1970, leaning on the farmgate outside the Rekisaari house; without nostalgia.

The rain all falls on the mainland she says and it was hard to find water for the garden – by which she means what I say too: a vegetable garden for feeding a family. It proved impossible in the end to stay summers in Ruotsalainen and visit the Rekisaari garden to water, daily across the sea to the northwest and still have time for fishing and the other things that make up island life. The Ilmalahtis live in this house all year now.

Until two years ago there was a fishing co-operative on this island; we see the smoke house for catches of Baltic herring just outside. The co-op is no more. When we can't understand his name for the herring traps, Sisko's husband draws us a picture with his biro of the box nets that are used to catch the herring – the anchors sit outside. The herring have their own traditions and have always run the same places when they arrive. The Ruotsalainen folk know their routes and it allows them to funnel the fish into an anchored box-frame lined with net, which is lifted when the shoal is inside.

Fish were smoked or salted and taken for sale at the annual fish fairs lasting a week in Helsinki and Turku.

With a decline in fish numbers, aggravated by State protection of seals here – a tourist attraction – Sisko estimates there are ten thousand seals in the archipelago, all of whom eat fish and raid and damage the box-traps, fishing is no longer a way to earn a living.

There's also the question of cormorants – we discover their name after a long description and a mime of a bird with wings outspread on a rock, drying for lack of sebaceous glands – the dinosaur looking bird. No-one knows the Englishing until after the mime: merimetsu in Finnish. They migrate in their thousands and eat the pike-perch. Wherever I go in the archipelago I'm given this name, but I'm none the wiser as to what species a pike-perch is.

It was seasonal work; the Baltic, being barely salty because of the influx of so much mainland river water and its lack of noticeable tides to flush it, freezes hard each winter.

As if a final nail were needed in island fishing economy, the small scale salmon farming proved susceptible to nitrates in the water from mainland crop growing practices. All the salmon now comes from Norway.

It's with a little regret, but a lot of pragmatism our conversation moves through all this. Ruotsalainen islanders are resourceful folk and maybe can see the days ahead through their oakwoods.

A faint sound of oak-song today, here in the island of trees and people growing together and growing old together, a backwash of events allowing enough time for the changes of that growth.

Thursday, 4 November 2010
Kurki

Quite simply then, sitting on the porch in dark frost-crackling night. Venus is there and a hooked edge of the moon.

I have the very last of the Campbeltown malt in my glass; I'm still barefoot after the sauna.

My eyes are cleansed of the day's grit – inner eye cleared of the grit of the day too. I'd set out to look for an oak forest towards Kustavi and found only a tunnel in the vuori – what Finns call a mountain –

a high expanse of bedrock. I'd walked in through burst steel gates in perpendicular rockface onto an earth floor along a tunnel carved through rock. There was a cracked-open fusebox. I followed the tunnel until the dark became absolute. The weapons- and oil-bunkers at Faslane came to mind and I became nervous and retraced my steps.

Barefoot with good malt here in the night and I'm surprised by the voices of geese – I know the geese have gone south – before I realise it's the bugling of cranes, who have a more restricted vocabulary than goose tribes. Bugling does it no justice: it's musical: there's a blare and a peal in it; a two note piping that echoes the day's tunnel.

One crane is warbling, momentarily rousing the others to call before they all shut off for the night. And I'm back to the medieval of Taivassalo kirk; the back of my neck prickles and then beyond Taivassalo's frescoes into the wild ancient mind where crane shrieks are omens.

Sibelius saw a crane flock two days before his death: "There they come, the birds of my youth."

Above and below Ainola, where Sibelius lived and died and above Saari and at the bay of Mietoisten the cranes fly and call still.

The archaic in our world is palpable in wetlands and woods; and is almost tangible in our wild minds.

Old men are boys again.

Monday, 8 November 2010
Habituation

Tammimäki is more than an oakwood on a wee hill as its name implies. More than a once-upon-a-time island in Mynämäki in south west Finland: part then of a still existing archipelago. It creeps up on me in the dark, sleeping in bed. It gets into the bed and lies down beside me. It's a state of mind – inserted somewhere between wakefulness of the small hours and night dreams. But then again, it's also daylight reverie.

But for the moment it's night. I navigate my way into the wood, careful not to step on the slender illuminated yearlings and saplings that somehow here seem to have escaped Oak Change and the fungus which helped the crisis along the way. I feel rather than see the elder and ancient trees around me. It's a small wood, with 35 or 36 such trees, five hundred and four hundred years in age, the oldest generation. They're all broken-limbed, wind-torn, leafless now, moon lighting the fabric of old wooden bone systems.

If I were to feel that there is a measure of acceptance now, cutting both ways, it would not be any form of anthropomorphism: rather a simple acknowledgement of fact. Sentient creatures are precisely that.

It's taken a long time to reach this point. I've slipped in and out of the wood for weeks. I've gratefully accepted, according to season, the mushrooms, the berries, the seeds and acorns the woodland produces; not for me or the deer, but for its own systemic purposes, its own continuing sustenance and existence. In the same way my body produces blood, but it's not for the benefit of mosquitoes.

I walk steadily and slowly round an inner meandering path of my own devising, assuring myself that each tree is in its rightful place, that each erratic boulder is in the place it found itself at the tongue of the last glacier. I step carefully over the fallen trees and round the raspberry tangles; more than once. And more than once realising that this is more than a vagary.

It's a dream; not because I'm asleep, which I'm not (though I'm not awake) but because the oaks are there at all. I'm visited now by these trees, just as I have visited for these months. It's a reverie not of my making, but one determined by my constant walking, by continued absorption – a word I use deliberately – of the woods and its internal structures and relationships, of which I am now a temporary part.

Sooner, perhaps rather than later, I'll pass along elsewhere in a way the oaks cannot, but part of me, the woodland flâneur, will always linger now in that small wood at the edge of the mainland on the Baltic; just as the oaks' wood, presence, timespan, timescale, has become a state of mind for me. Habituation. True dwelling. And it's here now in this very world and all its suffering.